LONGING IN
BELONGING

LONGING IN BELONGING

The Cultural Politics of Settlement

SUZAN ILCAN

 PRAEGER

Westport, Connecticut
London

Library of Congress Cataloging-in-Publication Data

Ilcan, Suzan.
    Longing in belonging : the cultural politics of settlement / Suzan Ilcan.
      p. cm.
    Includes bibliographical references and index.
    ISBN 0–275–96736–0 (alk. paper)
    1. Acculturation. 2. Group identity. 3. Human
settlements. 4. Immigrants. I. Title: Cultural politics of settlement. II. Title.
    HM841.I53 2002
     303.48'2—dc21   2001036703

British Library Cataloguing in Publication Data is available.

Library of Congress Catalog Card Number: 2001036703
ISBN: 0–275–96736–0

First published in 2002

Praeger Publishers, 88 Post Road West, Westport, CT 06881
An imprint of Greenwood Publishing Group, Inc.
www.praeger.com

Printed in the United States of America

The paper used in this book complies with the
Permanent Paper Standard issued by the National
Information Standards Organization (Z39.48–1984).

10 9 8 7 6 5 4 3 2 1

Copyright Acknowledgments

The author and publisher gratefully acknowledge permission for use of the following material:

Excerpts from *Transgressing Borders: Critical Perspectives on Gender, Household, and Culture*, edited by S. Ilcan and L. Phillips. Copyright © 1998 by S. Ilcan and L. Phillips. Reproduced with permission of Greenwood Publishing Group, Inc., Westport, CT.

Poetry by Fazil Hüsnü Dağlarca used by permission of Kemal Silay, Editor of the *Turkish Studies Association Bulletin*, Indiana University.

For Dan, Norma and Bülent

CONTENTS

ACKNOWLEDGMENTS

Many debts have been incurred in developing and preparing this work. I acknowledge with appreciation a research grant from the Social Sciences and Humanities Research Council of Canada that permitted me to carry out this project. I would like to thank the University of Windsor for providing travel funds which enabled me to present chapters of this book before various conference meetings, and for granting me a sabbatical leave in 2000–2001, which made it possible for me to complete the project during that extraordinary year. The University of Windsor's Sociology and Anthropology Department has provided a very supportive research environment for my work, and I am thankful for that.

Several people have generously contributed so much time, labor, and stimulation in helping with the development of this project. I would like to thank those people who, at various stages of the project's becoming, contributed to this book in different ways. I am extremely grateful to: Selma Eren for her outstanding research contributions to the project at many different stages, and for gently debriefing me on events occurring on the "outside"; Alper Özdemir for his meticulous arranging and processing of transcribed materials; and Debra Cady and Christiana Gauger for their skilful acquisitions and excellent library research. Over the years, drafts of many chapters have been discussed in seminars, workshops, and conferences that make it impossible to name everyone who helped improve the book. Nevertheless, a number of people should be singled out for notably helpful discussions, or for constructive comments on earlier sections or chapters of the book. In particular, I would like to acknowledge Tanya

Basok, Anthony Davis, Glynis George, Lynne Phillips, and Rob Shields for the intellectual challenges. I would also like to thank Dan O'Connor for stimulating discussions over the years, and for his honest and critical reading of the manuscript which has benefited in substantial ways. I thank Nira Yuval-Davis for the insightful presentation that she gave at the European Sociology Association meetings a few years ago and for her encouragement of my work at the time, both of which impelled me to locate concepts of migrancy and nation-building in the field of settlement practices. I would also like to thank the many writers I acknowledge in the text for not only inspiring me through their work, but for teaching me about the mobile dimensions of culture, place, and knowledge.

At Praeger Publishers, I am thankful to Dr. Jim Sabin for his confidence in the project from the beginning, and to David Palmer, Senior Production Editor, who has remained very supportive and helpful throughout the editorial stages. Also at Praeger, I would like to extend my appreciation to Jason Cook for the careful copyediting of the manuscript.

I acknowledge with great consideration the staff of many government and academic bodies in Turkey who generously provided materials or helped in other ways, and the Turkish authorities for granting me the permission to carry out the field research component of this project during my last visit in 1997. I remain indebted to Sema and Zeynep, and Ender G. and Tulu G., for their generosity, hospitality, and kindness, and for giving me a home away from home which I shall not forget.

My deepest appreciation and heartfelt gratitude go to those women and men in northwestern Turkey whose stories, struggles, and histories give life to the local and global ideas of settlement.

CHAPTER 1

INTRODUCTION

The globalizing era of rapid economic and cultural transformation has unsettled cultural locations and their settled ways. Those practices, beliefs, and ideas that were once considered folk culture and defined as organic expressions of locally lived experiences are, with ever increasing speed, being unsettled by the interconnectedness of the global milieu. Partly as a consequence of the expanded mobility of populations, and partly a consequence of the shifting of boundaries, the ideas and practices associated with belonging are under constant challenge. The home—with its attendant connotations of stability, constancy, and identity tied to the image of a locus of origination and habituated social ties—has become a contested and, for some, a mobile terrain. The mobility and mobilization of both populations and territories raises questions about the nature of the ties social groups have to their places, about the durability of these ties and the kind of settlement practices enacted for those on the move. In many cases, the locations of culture are imbued with uncertainty and insecurity by those who live a life of multiple border crossings (such as migrant workers, immigrants, and exiles), or those who inhabit the borderlands or who are considered marginal to their place. For those at the crossroads of displacement, for those who leave or who are forced to leave one home for another, and for those for whom belonging has been superseded by longing, there are risks involved. There are always risks associated with the journey of longing to belong, of a road that leads toward places less appealing than others and ends with the memories and losses incurred by the places left behind and all the paths forgone. As Bauman suggests, one cannot help suspect that no final and unambiguous judgment on the advantages or limitations of the journey chosen and followed will ever be fully obtained. The distress associated with having made a wrong move will precede and follow every step, now and in the future. While making one's own choices may be a liberating activity, this activity is also infilled with the tensions of "unsettlement" (1999, 160). For me, settlement is a practice without firm boundaries. Its enclosure is never complete or finalizable, as its boundaries are shot through with an enduring and unsettling tension. This tension is between being, and being otherwise. It takes the form of a longing that lingers with and within belonging—a longing that is both the motive and consequence of belonging and that which resists it. Longing is the inside thought from the outside. It is an outside thought that is in perpetual communication with the interiorities of settlement.

For people living with the tensions and consequences of globalization, deterritorialization, and mass migratory movements, "belonging" to a place, a home, or a people becomes not so much an insulated or individual affair as an experience of "being within and in-between sets of social relations" (Probyn 1996). This is not to suggest that the movement or displacement of people today is anything new—people have always been faced with living within and on the margins of social relations whether through pressure, choice, or contact with the forces of colonialism, modernity, or advanced liberalism. What is significant is that analysts (such as Kaplan 1998; Malkki 1999; Lovell 1998; Stewart 1996; Appadurai 1996; Gilroy 1993) are developing new conceptual frameworks to come to terms with the processes of displacement and have problematized conventional notions about the relationship between people and territory, identity and roots, or home and homelands. The idea of belonging to a "community," for example, is never simply the recognition of cultural similarity or social contiguity. It is instead a categorical identity that is characterized by various forms of exclusion and constructions of otherness (Gupta and Ferguson 1999a, 13). Similarly, the experience of being within and between sets of social relations also contributes to the characteristic of "modularity" in a multi-network society. Countering the ideal of homogeneous belongings, Bauman suggests that "none of the groups [to] which we enter do we belong 'fully': there are parts of our modular persons which 'stick out' and cannot be absorbed nor accommodated by any single group, but which connect and interact with other modules" (1999, 161). This condition of "modularity," with its lack of bolts, clamps, and rivets fastening the modules into a permanent shape, is a constant source of tension. The tension is especially heightened for migrants and displaced peoples, and for those who live in a world of diaspora. Belonging is integral to longing. On this issue, I am reminded of the way in which Probyn raises issues of the various longings for belonging. For her, belonging captures both the desire for some kind of attachment to other people, places, or modes of being, and the ways in which individuals and groups are caught within the interstices of wanting to belong. Belonging is fueled by yearning rather than by the positing of an identifiable goal or a stable state (1996, 19). The tension within belonging involves a generalized longing for a different way of life with different attachments or relations. In a condition of generalized displacement, longing remains diffuse and unstable and is therefore susceptible to various settlement strategies and ideologies of home and place.

In *Longing in Belonging: The Cultural Politics of Settlement*, I inquire into categories that are so often taken for granted, asking how and when home and homeland, travel and migration, habitation and movement, become critical cultural and political dimensions of people's lives. Explicit in this inquiry is an analysis of belonging and longing that takes nation-building, ethnographic practices, dwelling, and diaspora as mobile sites for exploring the cultural politics of settlement. The term "settlement" traditionally resonates with particular groups who come and settle in a "place"—such as refugee, migrant, and immigrant settlements or new settlements formed through assimilation, population planning, and development projects. However, no settlement is ever complete. It is always in a process of settling, unsettling, and resettling.

A settlement is a place where we live for a time. It may house particular groups, reflect patterns or practices of togetherness, and symbolize a past or present way of life. It should not be thought of as a permanent structure that has no openings or interchanges with the outside. There are always movements—of populations, of struggles, of ideas—that unsettle and resettle relations within, between, and beyond its borders. The mobility of populations, whether this includes the movement of migrant, immigrant, or refugee groups or the displacement of settled habits and beliefs, raises critical questions about belonging to a place. Belonging to a place is not an individual matter but an experience of being connected in and between sites of social relations. We may think here of the ways in which some groups "stick out" in a place and become involved in relations of social exclusion. They belong to a place but are not always accepted by others who live there. Their transitory tie to a place produces a longing in belonging. In this way, I think of settlement as involving forms of belonging and longing that connote ways in which particular groups are involved in *settling in* and *resettling* a place.

The emphasis on belonging and longing lends an urgency to questions about the politics of people's lives transformed in space and time: How do nation-states play a role in creating the conditions of belonging and longing for certain groups? How do particular social groups, such as those characterized as diasporic, make sense of their changing lives, and how do they articulate or challenge strategies of settlement? How do we, as researchers, understand and translate these articulations, and how do we connect them to other social events? If belonging and longing are alternative conceptions of viewing social relations, they are useful if they extend our analytical reach or if they permit other ways of envisioning and relating the various examples of people's complex histories and lives. I hope to show this analytical orientation through a number of historical and ethnographic case illustrations in the pages and chapters to follow.

Social and political institutions have long been implicated in developing schemes and plans of settlement and for defining homes for their respective populations. In many cases around the globe, emerging nation-states developed grand narratives of collective belonging in order to connect cultural distinctiveness with territory. As Borneman suggests, without both a territorial and a cultural identity, a people of a country can make no lawful claim to a national polity, and conversely, such a polity can make no legal claim to a people unless it delimits itself in territorial terms and delineates its people in cultural terms. In the context of nation-building and the creation of a German national identity, Borneman suggests that the link between territory and cultural identity is established when the citizens adopt official state categories for determining belonging or appropriate nation-state devices for defining group membership. For example, in the eighteenth century, the German nation-state sought to define citizenship in terms of the categories of membership in the *Haus* (house). With subsequent transformations in the polity, other membership categories emerged. During the Nazi period, administrators and politicians not only used marital and blood categories to determine Germanness, but also later employed scientific research on blood types to distinguish those who belonged—*Menschen* (humans)—from those who did not—*Untermenschen* (subhumans). These categories served to justify Nazi policies of internal purification and external expansion (1999).

The nation mobilizes cultural distinctiveness and the longing for belonging to a homeland in an effort to link particular groups to a territory while, at the same time, excluding other inhabitants or their cultural habits. This kind of orientation to nation-building, as expressed in the work of others (e.g., Bauman 1999; Cheah 1999; Gupta 1999; Yuval-Davis 2000), continues to inspire my interest in homelands and their interface with nationalism, modernity, and the rationalities of inclusion and exclusion. Throughout the span of my childhood and adolescence, this interest was perhaps initially stimulated by numerous trips to Turkey to visit relatives and friends during a time when the symbols of the "nation" were everywhere; homes, parks, schools, banks, and museums were then, as they are today, mottled with the icons used to animate the ongoing project of settlement called Turkish nationalism.

Through my interest in the Middle East and my research in Turkey, I have come to understand nation-building as a process of creating a past and present, inventing new traditions, and constructing new rationalities and categories of belonging for various groups. In some nation-building efforts, this process involved strategies for displacing people from their past to produce a longing as well as a series of directives to lead the diaspora to new images of home and new cultural practices for belonging. In chapter 2, in the context of the literature on the cultural politics of nation-building in the Middle East and elsewhere, I illustrate how the development of nation-building hinges on the production of things imagined and symbolized through a process of creating the "home of a nation" and the "nation as a home." I situate this discussion in one of the modern reform projects that emerged historically in Turkey around the time of the formation of the Republic in 1923. I argue that this reform movement attempted to limit the vestiges of the semicolonial Ottoman Empire. It employed ways for the new nation to appear "modern" so as to make a place for itself (and its citizens) among other modern European nation-states in the future. As a way to displace the existing monuments of Ottoman tradition and find a new home for itself in the global world, the nation-state introduced new categories to resettle the lives of its citizens and their habitats. These categories, in the form of codes, ranged from the formal separation of the state from religion, the adoption of the Italian Penal Code, the adoption of the Swiss Civil Code to replace the Islamic code of law, to the replacement of the Arabic script by the then newly scripted Latin-based Turkish alphabet. In addition to these political and cultural transformations, this nation-state, like other European and Middle Eastern nation-states, deployed concepts of gender and family, as well as new images of the "house," in its nation-building efforts. Primarily through their visibility, publicity, and cultural production, notions of gender and family became central instruments (and sites of contest) in propelling a new homeland and settlement. Locating gender or family within the boundaries of nation-building reflects one way that this nation-state promoted particular social categories for the purposes of social change. Nation-building efforts, here and elsewhere, involve the mobilization of categories for generating cultural portrayals of homeland.

For those who endeavor to make sense of contemporary processes of cultural production in an era of transnationalism or globalization, a focus on the mobilization of categories of displacement and migration introduces an array of ethnographic possibilities. Categories of displacement and migration as well as habitation and movement are entwined in studies of cultural production and are central to the contemporary ethnography or the "new ethnography." Perhaps more than anything else, the emphasis on the mobilization of categories emanates from my ethnographic experiences of dwelling in a variety of "home" places and from my mobile, rather than stationary, relations to these places and their equally mobile inhabitants. It is with this background in mind that I inquire into the relationship among ethnographic practices, mobile populations, and places in transit and transition.

In chapter 3, in drawing upon a wide range of ethnographic insights and my own ethnographic experiences of traveling and dwelling at home and abroad, I show how the concept of movement—its related styles of travel and migration, its interface between the local and the global, location and displacement—twists and spirals its way into the ethnographic practices of reading, remembering, writing, and retelling. I understand movement not in relative terms, in the way that practices of ethnography move from point to point in a specific field, but in terms of how it operates within unsettled and variable fields that allow for fluid dimensions of culture to come more sharply into view. If movement is taken into serious account by researchers, it may well serve to alert us to a form of ethnographic research that neither focuses on one bounded place nor offers a view of "people" as unproblematically belonging to a place. This mobile orientation opens up multiple territories of inquiry (as opposed to firmly anchored situations) and recognizes how ethnographic practices—of "writing against culture" (Abu-Lughod 1993), listening and translating (Phillips 1996), remembering and retelling (Cole 1998; Stewart 1996), and resisting to view "culture as noun" (Appadurai 1996)—are related to the many mobile dimensions that operate within ethnography. Such an orientation not only turns away from mapping "culture" in place and time, but also examines the displacement of the ethnographer "in the field." It alerts me to a wide range of social practices, stories, and events that reflect lives in transit and transition. Moreover, it recognizes that all connections of place, people, and culture are social and historical creations to be explained, rather than facts that contain or constrain.

My perspective on the mobile dimensions of culture has been informed by many contemporary and critical ethnographies, including a wide range of recent and provocative research that highlights the necessity of interrelating dimensions of culture and not categorizing "cultures" as wholes or separate entities (e.g., Bridgman, Cole, and Howard-Bobiwash 1999; Gupta and Ferguson 1999a; Malkki 1999; Rapport and Dawson 1998; Clifford 1997). A focus on the interrelations of dimensions of culture occurs at a time when cultural distinctiveness is becoming increasingly unsettled because of the mass migrations and transnational cultural flows of a global, capitalist world. The twentieth century has, in fact, witnessed the development of a global environment to the point that domestic and national spaces have become increasingly deterritorialized (see Sassen 1998). Within such transformations, an unprecedented number of people (such as refugees) have fled their homes to escape famine, genocide, or persecution. Other large groups of people have moved around the globe in search of paid employment or to overcome the devastating consequences of conflict back home. And still other groups, considered by governments and communities to be the local "foreigners," have faced forceful assimilation and ethnic cleansing, as well as other similar methods deployed by local state powers to keep them in check or move them back to "where they came from." These events and relations have drawn my attention to issues of diaspora as they relate to people's practices of settlement and their forms of belonging and longing.

The subject of diaspora is massive—historically, geographically, and culturally. References to movement, transit, migrancy, displacement, and homelands flood the analyses of diaspora in contemporary sociological, anthropological, and cultural criticism. Such analyses include critical assessments of conservative approaches to territory and borders; criticisms of essentialist notions of culture; the politics of origins and nativeness; and examinations of the dispersion of peoples from homelands and the experiences of "otherness" that follow with it. I approach the notion of diaspora as one involving processes of unsettlement and movement. These are processes that are experienced by people who are forced to migrate from their homeland or who are drawn into new places to live for economic or political reasons. These new places require new habits and responsibilities for those whose aim is to settle in these alien environments.

The path of inquiry that I take in chapter 4 involves assessing how the notion of diaspora underscores the combined cultural and political relations of migration and otherness that characterize particular displaced and uprooted peoples. I offer many examples and outcomes of diaspora within the context of twentieth-century migrant populations. Here I examine the post–World War II diasporic "guest workers" in Europe. I focus on the guest worker system in Germany and draw attention to issues relating to the recruitment of workers to host countries; the bilateral agreements between Germany and the sending countries; and the regulation of guest workers through policies and programs that control their place and status. I extend this focus to include an analysis of the largest group of guest workers in Germany, those who are from Turkey and who are now referred to as *Ausländer*. The marginality of this group is not only due to its relations with the economic system of the host country, but it is also manifest in its cultural distinctiveness. Their cultural distinction as diaspora is reflected in their personal and poetic descriptions of their location in *gurbet*, that is, in their perceived state of exile, and in their longing for belonging. As Kaplan puts it, exile is "always already a mode of dwelling at a distance from a point of origin" (1998, 143). This mode of dwelling is also experienced by those who live in their national homelands but who are nevertheless displaced. Here I refer to inmarrying women and other itinerant groups who move through the nation. Based upon a wide array of diasporic articulations, I argue that diaspora neither develops from rooted communities nor is it a property of individuals or groups in isolation. Instead, it is through combined processes of migration and "othering" that these diasporas are constituted. Diasporic groups remember and relay the outcomes of these processes in the stories that they tell and from the vantage point of experiencing a politics of marginality.

My enduring academic interest in people's lives "on the margins" is inspired by my communication and contact with immigrant groups and in-marrying women in northwestern Turkey, particularly in the community of Arzu.[1] Through their displacement, I have learned how precarious and arbitrary, and yet how powerful, such categories of belonging are. In chapter 5, I illustrate how belonging in this community serves to configure social relations historically and materially. Following from the insights of Probyn (1996) and Bauman (2001a), I emphasize how belonging is not so much a secured and individual affair as an experience of living within and on the margins of social relations in a world of increasing insecurity and uncertainty. As a starting point, I introduce the historical and political complexities connected with Turkish immigrants living in Bulgaria and their subsequent return to various parts of Turkey during the years between the formation of the Republic in 1923 and World War II. Members of this diaspora resettled their families and their lives in Arzu. Through the assistance of the Turkish state, they made new homes for themselves. I delineate the relations of diapora that this group encountered in what they now consider their homeland. These relations are elaborated through their own detailed stories and memories of belonging. On the basis of my presence as a participant in their stories and as a listener and writer, with all the complications that such a presence transmits, I argue that these stories give us insight into the comforting, yet sometimes disturbing, features of settlement practices. Arzu is not a confined place of solitude or seclusion, nor are its social arrangements fixed as a consequence. It is a place that is not bound by its past or its present; instead it exists in duration as the diasporic relations of Arzu continually form and transform through processes of division, differentiation, and designation. It is unsettled by numerous crises and transient passages that move through its borders and divisions and render them fragile and pervious to forces of change. Arzu provides an evocative site from which to consider the specificity and mutations of movement in relation to outside practices and places of settlement.

Settlements—nations, neighborhoods, dwellings—embody cultural dimensions of order or discipline that stand against other forms of social cohesion. They are, however, never without the small movements of longing and belonging that challenge the order of things. Settlements are sites of difference that may be uprooted by political and cultural struggles initiated by their very own inhabitants. I am not referring to the predictable or regulated activities of dwelling that take place under specific conditions with determinable effects. I am instead referring to the unexpected, to the indeterminacy of uncontainable change that takes place on the margins. Without having to delve too deeply here into the voluminous literature on the cultural politics of dwelling, my point is to introduce the notion of movement within belonging. Following Probyn, this is movement that seeks not a direct road but instead gathers up recollections, stories, sayings, and other things along its way. It is a method of connection and links between things and ways of being that rearranges common perspectives on settlement and habitation. I think here of the complex, yet subtle, ways in which alternative relations of belonging are created by those who change their home without moving anywhere. These relations include events and the emergence of new alignments seemingly impossible within the architectures of order and discipline. Such alternative relations of belonging are everywhere—in shadows of the day-to-day and the interstices of relations of power, the implications and consequences of which are outside the spaces of predictability and regulation. Their presence cannot be fully self-present lest they be subsumed or appropriated by the powers that be.

To offer one possible line of analysis of alternative relations of belonging, I consider how particular social arrangements transform and displace the household and its settlement practices. In chapter 6, I begin by assessing those sedentary or settled places that have been known to individualize and direct groups of people according to regulated time, distinct labor divisions, and institutionalized modes of belonging. In the ethnographic context of Arzu, I illustrate how disciplinary spaces, such as households, settle people (most notably women) into particular ways of living by dividing and combining their activities into established totalities. In these all-too-visible spaces, women merely appear as immobile subjects and victims of institutional structures. Articulating Braidotti's notion of transdisciplinarity (1994) and Abu-Lughod's notion of "writing against culture" (1993), I explore how a nomadic orientation is useful for challenging rigid institutional views of settlement and for understanding how women create space and time for themselves. This space and this time are marked by the collective and recollective efforts of coming together, of interconnections, and of storytelling. These stories are not simply told and then forgotten; they are expressed by those who have a sharpened sense of settlement or territory. They are stories that contain an inherent element of newness and dynamism: they disrupt the sequencing of the dominant order by confronting local customs. They compel alliances among women and convey a critical awareness of the workings of power. I argue that these and other such social practices force people to reconsider how disciplinary spaces are lived and how influential these practices of settlement are in provoking social change.

Settlement entails questions of belonging and longing. These processes engage all of us in different ways and with various implications. They continue to have a place in events and therefore require us to bring them to the fore in our analytical thinking. My concern is to show the interrelationship between the dimensions of culture, the processes involved in transfiguring locations, and the mobile practices that inform our relations to home and to other cultural and political fields. In the chapters that follow, I will trace out the tensions that mobilize these relationships with the aim of moving beyond the stasis associated with settlement and revealing, through an analysis of settlement practices, the possibilities inherent in these practices.

NOTE

1. The fieldwork carried out in northwestern Turkey, particularly in the community of Arzu (pseudonym) during the spring and summer months of 1996, was made possible by a grant from the Social Sciences and Humanities Research Council of Canada (SSHRCC). Previous fieldwork conducted in northwestern Turkey, particularly in Saklı (pseudonym), from August 1988 to September 1989, was made possible by a doctoral fellowship funded by SSHRCC.

CHAPTER 2

MIGRANT NATIONALISM

For the late twentieth century, nationalism is likely one of the few examples that we associate most closely with violence, destruction, and death. The end of the millennium has been marked by a register of ethnic expulsions, fundamentalist intolerance, and genocidal devastations. These practices, often dressed as a "defense of law and order" (Bauman 2001a), are widely regarded as excessive articulations of nationalism. Among the catalog of related incidences, we can recall the German resettlement policies and internal cleansing practices that resulted in the genocide of Jewish inhabitants, the treatment of the Yanomami in the context of the Brazilian national polity, and the violence against guest workers living in Western Europe or ethnic minorities living in "homelands." Indeed, one might venture to suggest, as Cheah (1999) does, that nationalism has become the model design of death. However, to nationalism's seemingly inescapable affinity with violence and death we must also add a paradoxical corollary: nationalism is also seemingly inseparable from the longing for life and is inextricably tied to the ongoing processes of nation-building.

In a variety of nationalist discourses, the nation is compared to a living organic being and understood as a medium through which individuals can secure a life beyond violence and death. The nation, in other words, is a site that guarantees an eternal future for its citizens and for the generations of citizens that follow (see Cheah 1999, 176). In reflecting on nationalism as nation-building, I regard nationalism as a process of imagining a past and present (Anderson 1991, 1983), of inventing traditions (Hobsbawn and Ranger 1983), and of designing a place for new categories of groups and communities. Through rationalities of inclusion and exclusion, nation-building efforts both differentiate and homogenize local communities and traditions into an image of nation as a living entity that will endure and promote life in the future. Embarking on this journey toward life in the future is a process of unsettling and resettling a place in time. Nation-building efforts are coercive resettlement practices. They are a variety of symbolic social movements that displace and pass through time. They change locations without necessarily going anywhere. In this symbolic journey from one home to another, the pressing concern is what to include and exclude, that is, what to take and what to leave behind. These departure plans will effect both the rapidity of transit and the ease of resettlement. The speed of transit, even through time, always varies in relation to the weight of encumbrances while the fluency of settlement varies with the availability of resources for making a new home. These encumbrances and resources are the symbolic goods of nation-building settlement practices. For nations are, as Bauman claims, "abstract-imagined-totalities" (1999, 36). Their symbols hover high above the world of immediate, face-to-face, personal experience as they embark on a journey of reconfiguring cultural memories. Symbols encourage citizens what to remember or forget about the past, and what new values will service the homeland in its desire for perpetuity.

The nation is not a coherent and cohesive, self-enclosed, self-sustained totality or bounded entity with clearly expressed and closely interlocked elements. I view the nation as a location of difference and transformation. It is a project rather than an entity. Developing the insights of Gupta (1999), for me the study of nation-building involves studying phenomena that transgress "the national order of things" and the processes and strategies that link social groups, like that of gender, to the symbols and practices of belonging to a nation. What interests me is how the location called "nation" involves a movement that creates a new order of difference, a new alignment of location in relation to other "nations," other communities, and other homelands. In creating this new order of difference, nation-building efforts often involve transforming popular beliefs into superstitions, popular habits into symbols of uncivility, or popular lifestyles into signs of a "lack of culture" (Bauman 1999, 103; 2000).

While all nation-building efforts share common features, each nation unfolds its project in an historically specific field and develops a distinct style for anticipating and directing its future home. In this chapter I want to illustrate the ways in which nation-building projects undertaken by the Turkish state in the early twentieth century hinged on the production of things imagined and symbolized in order to make the "home of a nation" and to make the "nation a home." Drawing upon the literature on the cultural politics of nation-building in the Middle East and elsewhere, I analyze various aspects of nation-building projects in Turkey after the national independence war of 1919–1923 and following the formation of the Republic in 1923 by Mustafa Kemal (Atatürk)[1] and his reformers. I suggest that this resettlement movement brought the cultural vestiges of the colonial Ottoman Empire into a symbolic conflict with the plans to remake Turkey into a modern nation and to make it at home with the other nation-states of Western Europe. In this regard, the nation is not simply a facticity but a set of mobilizing plans and strategies; it is not a ready-made totality but a totalizing symbolic project.

In analyzing any nation-building project, it is important to focus not only on its stated goals and specific targets but also on the sites where these mobilizing strategies are applied. I argue that it is in these local sites that modern images are constructed and nation-building, modernity, and gender intersect. Understood in terms of its application, Turkey's early nation-building project was not homogeneous and did not proceed without resistance. I suggest that dimensions of the practices of gender and family, and their relations to the home and the homeland, were perceived as both obstacles and central symbolic resources to be mobilized in this movement. In the 1920s, both gender practices and family relations were sites wherein the struggle between empire and nation were played out. These practices and relations were significant because of their visibility, dispersion, mobility, and publicity. In conjunction with other visual practices that aimed to publicize the new nation-state, both gender and family practices were used in disseminating modern appearances and habits to the members of society at large and to the European West.

A HOME OF NATION-BUILDING

> As a cultural ideal, nationalism is the claim that while men and women have many identities, it is the nation that provides them with their primary form of belonging.
>
> As a moral ideal, nationalism is an ethic of heroic sacrifice, justifying the use of violence in the defense of one's nation against enemies, internal or external.
>
> —M. Ignatieff, *Blood and Belonging* (1993, 5)

Much has been written on the transformation of traditional society to modern society. Some scholars, such as Giddens, have argued that the modern social order came into being, as a consequence of "detraditionalizing forces," to highlight the uprooting effects of capitalist production on local communities, customs, and practices (1994, 84). There is little doubt that the spread of capitalist relations uprooted particular local economies and their cultural dimensions in diverse ways. Turkey is no exception. The expansion of capitalist production facilitated a decline in the authoritarianism of landlord–peasant relations (see chapter 5), forced the movement of rural populations to urban centers to sell their labor power, and promoted new gendered conceptions of work, time, and space. However, aside from the "detraditionalizing" influences of the development of capitalist relations, in what follows I explore the early "modernizing" strategies carried out by the Turkish nation-state, particularly by the Kemalist movement from the early 1920s to the early 1930s. These modern strategies were built around displacing the monuments of the past (such as Islamic symbols and religious time, as well as traditional forms of education, language, and fashion) from their positions of privilege and influence, and replacing them with signs of the future (Western civil codes, systems of rights, built environments, Western time and fashion). Hence, these strategies of displacement were critical in building the nation-state and Turkish nationalism. Both territorial sovereignty and cultural distinctiveness are complicitous with nationalism (see Brodie 2000a; Borneman 1999). The strategy of Turkish nationalism practiced during this period privileged the future over a past. It identified the monuments of Ottoman life and its religious cosmology as both burdensome and antithetical to the desired speed and direction of the Kemalist movement.[2]

Monuments of the Past, Signs of the Future

> Nationalism breeds . . . endemic nervousness in nations it spawns. It trains the nations in the art of vigilance that means a lot of restlessness and promises no tranquillity; it makes the nationhood into a task always to be struggled for and never to be fulfilled in the degree justifying the complacency that comes with victory. It creates the state of permanent tensions of which it presents itself as the solution; it thrives on that tension, it draws from it its life juices.
> —Z. Bauman, "Soil, Blood and Identity" (1992, 687–688)

Mustafa Kemal, the first president of the Republic of Turkey, and his Republican People's Party (RPP) attempted to create a new Turkish nation from the vestiges of the multiethnic, multinational, Ottoman Empire. Ottoman culture was diverse. It was characterized by a spirit of cosmopolitanism, by ethnic, linguistic, and religious mixture and interchange.[3] Though pale in comparison with the height of the Empire, the existing ruling class was made up of a group of large landowners (the *ayans, derebeys,* and *agas*) who owned the majority of arable land, and a group of urban merchants of mainly minority ethnic origin (Greek and Armenian) who controlled import–export trade and the domestic market for European imports (Berberoğlu 1991, 275). The national movement spurred on by the Kemalists and consisting primarily of bureaucrats, military personnel, middle-class urban dwellers, and town traders aimed to challenge both the spirit and the diversity of Ottoman culture and the hegemony of the existing ruling class.

At the end of World War I the remnants of Ottoman military power were finally defeated as the Anatolian provinces were occupied by the Allied powers. Greek forces landed in Izmir in May 1919 and Istanbul and other areas were subsequently occupied by European troops, including the British, French, and Italian forces. The occupation by the Allied powers unleashed protests in which both women and men joined (Kandiyoti 1991, 37; Moghadam 1993, 81). Drawing their momentum from the protests over Allied occupation, the Kemalists, under the leadership of Mustafa Kemal, began a War of National Independence in Anatolia in 1919. Within a few years, the Kemalists seized power and announced the establishment of the Turkish Republic in 1923. With flagging industrial production, disintegrating international trade networks, and disrupted agricultural production, the task of rebuilding Turkey was foremost on the political agenda. To redress the problems confronting the region, the Kemalist movement aimed to transform Turkey into a modern nation-state. For Mustafa Kemal this meant that: "We cannot shut ourselves in within our boundaries and ignore the outside world. We shall live as an advanced and civilised nation in the midst of contemporary civilization" (cited in Ahmad 1993, 53). Developing a national economy meant nationalizing the foreign-owned railway system, converting the Ottoman tobacco monopoly into a state monopoly, improving the financial infrastructure, establishing industrial relations as the economic base, and promoting new forms of economic development in urban and rural areas. Developing a national political culture meant integrating the ideologies and symbols of nationalism with modernism and the equality of rights for women. These nation-building efforts were considered necessary elements in the struggle to bring Turkey in line with other contemporary European nations.[4]

Whether the narratives and symbols of nationalism succeed depends a great deal on the practices of state institutions. The nation is continually represented in such state institutions as courts, schools, bureaucracies, and museums and in the icons and symbols of the nation: flags, currency, seals, and national artists, architects, intellectuals, and novelists (see Gupta 1999; Urry 2000). But nationalism is also constituted by a state's external dealings with other states, that is, with states that recognize and validate these practices as belonging to an entity that is similar in kind. Externally oriented practices—such as marking borders, maintaining embassies in one another's countries, signing treaties, declaring war, gaining admission to the United Nations—are partly responsible for validating ideologies of nationalism (Gupta 1999, 192). These are some of the practices through which the "nation" is represented in and to other nation-states. There are, however, other practices through which the nation is imagined and represented.

In Turkey, nation-building practices ranged from disparaging past traditional practices to borrowing codes from other nation-states. During the early years of the Republic, the Kemalists' primary concern was instituting political and social reforms. Drawing from the rhetoric of the times, the Kemalist movement depreciated the Ottoman past for its "backwardness." Its religiosity and imperial culture were considered the source of social, cultural, and economic stagnation. Religiosity was seen as a subversive force that posed a threat to modernization and nationalization processes, and so began a systematic attack on the institutions and practices belonging to Ottoman lifestyles: the office of the Caliphate (spiritual head of the Islamic religion) and the religious courts were abolished and all members of the Ottoman dynasty were ordered out of the country in 1924, one year after the proclamation of the Republic (Zurcher 1993, 175). Until 1926, the Şeriat, the Islamic code of law, was used to control betrothal, heterosexual marriage, divorce, inheritance, and adoption practices. Exceptions were made and various religious communities were able to define their own laws pertaining to family and inheritance. The replacement of the Şeriat by the Kemalist-adopted Swiss Civil Code in 1926 abolished the jurisdiction of Islamic hegemony over family relations and brought family life under the jurisdiction of secular codes. In the same year the Italian Penal Code was adopted from Mussolini's Italy and a Commercial Code, derived from German and Italian business practice, was instituted (see Kandiyoti 1991, 22; Jayawardena 1986). In 1926 the lunar Islamic calendar, which began in the year when the Prophet Muhammad migrated from Mecca to Medina, was replaced by the Georgian calendar. Even the Islamic way of keeping time, in which the day began and ended with the call to prayer, made way for the international clock. Changing the records of time was part of a movement to align the Republic with Europe and to facilitate international communication, especially in matters of business (Ahmad 1993, 80).

These changes were followed by the abolition of the Ministry of Religious Affairs and Pious Foundations, the closure of medrese (religious education), the proscription of male religious headgear (the fez), and the dissolution of the dervish orders (terikats, or mystical brotherhoods). Between 1928 and 1935, other radical reforms were passed, including the disestablishment of the state religion in 1928; the replacement of the Arabic script by a newly designed, Latin-based, Turkish alphabet in 1928; the establishment of girls institutes to educate young females on modern aspects of homemaking formed under the Ministry of Education in 1928;[5] the establishment of "National Schools" for teaching the new language to adults in 1929;[6] and the use of the Turkish language in place of Arabic in the Islamic call to prayer in 1932. Likewise, in 1935, Sunday replaced Friday as the weekly holiday, bringing the Turkish working week in line with that of the West (see Ahmad 1993). The changes spawned by the Kemalist movement traversed a huge amount of space-time as the migration from a society of tradition to a nation-state compelled along at great speed.

By replacing the monuments of tradition—the symbols of common heritage believed to be shared by a nation's peoples—with signs of modernity, the movement was giving its people the keys that would permit the nation to pass from the past to the future, from East to West, from tradition to modernity. While these new codes of conduct, or what Bourdieu (1993) would call "cultural capital," may well have provided some people with the know-how or the competence to decipher and participate in modern culture, they were initially designed to give the impression that the nation-state and its peoples had radically transformed their ways. The past was not worthy of imitation, and whatever was still visible about it was out of place in the new regime. The distaste of the past was echoed in one of Mustafa Kemal's speeches in the 1920s:

we are going to be civilized and be proud of it. Look at the rest of the Turks and Muslims! What catastrophes and disasters have come upon them, because their minds could not adjust themselves to the all-encompassing and sublime dictates of civilization! This is why we too remained backward for so long, and why we were stuck in the last swamp. If we have been able to save ourselves in the last few years, it has been because of the change in our mentality. We can never stop again. . . . We must go on; we have no choice. The nation must understand this clearly. Civilization is a blazing fire so powerful that it burns and annihilates all those who are indifferent to it. (Atatürk 1952, 207)

The use of "civilization" in this passage clearly alerts us not only to the divide between civilized and uncivilized but to the relationship between civilized and the demand for change in people's orientation. In another speech, Mustafa Kemal emphasized the relationship between the new script and the civilizing process:

Our rich and harmonious language will now be able to display itself with new Turkish letters. We must free ourselves from these incomprehensive signs that for centuries have held our minds in an iron cage. You must learn the new Turkish letters quickly. Teach them to your compatriots, to women and to men, to porters and to boatmen . . . for a nation to consist of 80 percent of illiterates is shameful. Now is the time to eradicate the errors of the past. . . . Our nation will show, with its script and with its mind that its place is with the civilized world. (cited in Lewis 1968, 124)

The logic of western modernization had come to be seen as necessary and inevitable and the discourses of the reformers centered around "catching up" with "civilization." The nation-state as a modern project was conceived as "the project of civilization," a project that involved the transformation of Muslim traditional social organization and ways of life (Göle 1997, 63). By subverting the old habits of society and concretizing new patterns of custom and lifestyle, the Kemalist reformers attempted to create what Bourdieu (1993) would call a new *habitus* (see Göle 1996, 65).

This new *habitus* would allow the nation's peoples to infiltrate the "modern" world and presumably flourish there. Such a project also meant embracing the "habits" of modernity in politics, administration, law, culture, and education. This would also entail improving the rights of women and adopting appropriate dress codes. Notwithstanding changes in scientific knowledge, built environments, Western-styled customs, and other such preferences, changes in gender relations were among the most controversial of all reforms. The clothing of men and women, the determination of space allocation for men and women, and the regulation of relations between the genders were focal points of the regime.

Turkey's nation-building efforts in its early modern period parallel the way other nation-builders engaged both in writing the history of the "nation" by stretching into the distant past and in protecting their fragile sovereignty by employing nationalist discourses and practices within their territories (see Gupta 1999, 189). There is a sense here that nation-building attempts aim to homogenize the varying accounts of community while, paradoxically, accentuating their differences. According to Gupta, nationalism assembles into its fold the disseminated historical narratives of various and often unrelated communities. Additionally, nationalist narratives also recognize and sometimes celebrate difference. The recognition that different ethnic groups, different locales, and different communities and religions have each their own role to play in the national project underscores their differences at the same time that it homogenizes and embodies them (1999, 191; see also Ertem 1999). The emphasis on homogenizing particular communities through nation-building has occurred in the early formation of a variety of nationalism efforts. Communities of gender and family are prime examples of the way in which these social groupings are both incorporated and differentiated within projects of nation-building.

Gender and Nation-Building

What is the relationship between nation-building projects and gender? Why is the question of women, in particular, integral to nation-building and other reform movements? How are images of gender used in such political platforms and what are the consequences? These are some of the questions that have been shaping my thinking about the relationship between gender and modernity in the context of nation-building. They are also questions that some contemporary researchers continue to pose when analyzing particular kinds of reform movements, such as those of nationalism, revolution, and Islamization. But, and as Moghadam (1994, 1–2) argues, each of these reform movements has a prolific body of traditional literature that carries with it a silence on issues of gender. Even the vast literature on nations and nationalism rarely concentrates on the question of gender. Yet it is becoming increasingly clear that discourses and reform laws pertaining to gender and notions of femininity and masculinity are central to the political and cultural projects of many reform movements, both past and present. Though, this gender connection does not necessarily mean that women and men are similarly connected to or equally identified with reform movements generally or with nationalism in particular. Rather, studies show that gender and nationalism affect each other and culminate in shifting forms of social relationships that are based on ethnicity, sexuality, and family (e.g., Probyn 1999; Stasiulis 1999; Yeğenoğlu 1998; Yuval-Davis 1997; Z. Arat 1994; Enloe 1989; Anthias and Yuval-Davis 1989; Yuval-Davis and Anthias 1989).

A frequently cited example of the disparity between the goals of national liberation and the outcome for women is the Algerian war of independence against the French in 1954. In Algeria, despite the participation of upwards of ten thousand women in the national liberation struggle, their future status was already shaped by the needs of male revolutionaries to restore Arabic as the primary language, Islam as the religion of the state, and women as the sovereigns of the family (Knauss 1987). After independence, the claims of Ben Bella (the country's first president) concerning the status of women never materialized, although his words sounded promising: "The Algerian women, who played an important role in the revolution, must play the same role in the construction of our country. We oppose those who, in the name of religion, wish to leave our women outside of this construction" (cited in Gordon 1968, 62). As Ahmed argues, the freedoms gained for Algerian women during their participation in the nationalist struggle were temporary (1982, 165). In fact, from the early 1960s to 1984, a long struggle persisted around codifying and formalizing the relationship between women and men in the family domain. Against the backdrop of women being removed from formal political settings and confined to a women's organization (Union Nationale des Femmes Algeriennes) under the leadership of the National Liberation Front, the single-party Algerian state adopted the Family Code in 1984. According to Bouatta (1994, 23), "the text of this law, inspired by the Sharia, officially establishes women in a position of inferiority, and establishes the dominance of men in matters concerning marriage, divorce, inheritance, and so on." In this regard, both gender and home are the sites, among other sites, for expressing nationalism.

While women in Algeria (as well as in Iran and Turkey) played a critical role in nation-building efforts, this did not prevent them from being marginalized (ideologically and politically) in the public world of work and politics following independence. As Abdo puts it, "in almost all liberation movements where women were actively involved, a general reversal of their roles became the fact of life after national liberation and the establishment of the nation-state" (1994, 150). This kind of discrepancy for women prevailed even though in some nation-states, as Jayawardena (1986) shows, there was a compatibility between nation-building and women's struggles for equality and a relationship between national identity and gender.

In what follows, I will explore how the Turkish modernity project scripted and conscripted a new character: the new, modern woman who would span the gulf between the past and future and would be responsible for moving the population to its new home. While the traditional woman was perceived to be lacking in public rights, recognition, and education, the new, modern woman was to be educated, dedicated to her family, and concerned with national interests (see Najmabadi 1993, 493). However, the outcome of the movement to produce modern women was not always true to its aim.

Scripting the "New Woman" As a National Symbol

One of the most important mechanisms for representing the "deep horizontal comradeship" that one citizen feels for another is the mass media (Anderson 1983, 16). In Anderson's view, the ability to imagine the nation is closely tied to print capitalism and technology. Newspapers enable the nation to be represented by the juxtaposition of stories, from different regions, and to be assimilated under one date; similarly, the nation is differentiated from others by the presentation of "international" and "foreign" news (see Gupta 1999, 187). I would also suggest that other media outlets, particularly public speeches, are important mechanisms for spreading the values associated with belonging to a nation.[7]

The proliferation of new media outlets—from newspapers and coffee houses to public speeches—produced the central mechanisms for establishing the legitimacy of nation-building in Turkey. Public speeches, similar to newspapers and having similar mass media effects, are opportunities for imagining the nation. Mustafa Kemal, for example, made several speeches in various regions of the country, in which he valorized the ideals of European Enlightenment thought: the ideals of progress, freedom, and equality. In these speeches, he supported improving the rights of women. It was repeatedly emphasized that the education of women was important for achieving the well-being of the nation and the desired level of civilization. The linking of modernization to women was evident in a speech he delivered in Izmir in 1923: "A civilization where one sex is supreme can be condemned, there and then, as crippled. A people that has decided to go forward and progress must realize this as quickly as possible. The failures in our past are due to the fact that we remained passive to the fate of women" (cited in Yeğenoğlu 1998, 132). Additionally, he drew public attention to women as civic entities. In Izmir, Konya, Inebolu, and Kastamonu he spoke of the hope for a revolution in the status of women. His newly founded Republic, he said, would create a government in which everyone, men and women alike, would have equal rights. In a speech delivered in Izmir in 1923, he said that "the weakness of Turkish society lies in our indifference to the status of women" (cited in Taşkiran 1976, 55–56). With the nation requiring science and knowledge, he argued that women and men must share in these pursuits equally. In his Kastamonu speech, the ideal of equality between the sexes was deemed necessary for achieving the desired level of progress:

Let us be frank: society is made of women as well as men. If one grants all the rights to progress to the one and no rights at all to the other, what happens? Is it possible that one half of the population is in chains for the other half to reach the skies? Progress is possible only through a common effort, only thus can the various stages be by-passed. (cited in Yeğenoğlu 1998, 132)

In the same context, Mustafa Kemal also stressed the importance of motherhood and its ties to nation-building:

The most important duty of women is motherhood. The importance of this duty is better understood, if one considers that the earliest education takes places on one's mother's lap. Our nation had decided to be a strong nation. Circumstances today require the advancement of our women in all respects. Therefore, our women, too, will be enlightened and learned, and like men, will go through all educational stages. Then, women and men, walking side by side, will be each other's help and support in social life. (cited in Jayawardena 1986, 36)

Motherhood did not conflict with the national interests of change and progress. In their capacity as reproducers, women were linked to the future of the nation as the socializers of the next generation of citizens. As an emblem of reproductive heterosexuality and continuity, motherhood was imagined as the agency responsible for advancing toward the nation-state. But motherhood also required additional and more advanced qualifications for women. In Mustafa Kemal's words:

As time passes, science progresses, and civilization advances with giant steps, so increases the difficulties of raising children according to the necessities of life in this country, and we are aware of this. The education that mothers have to provide to their children today is not simple, as it had been in the past. Today's mothers have to attain several high qualities in order to bring up children with the necessary qualities and develop them into active members for life today. Therefore, our women are obliged to be more enlightened, more prosperous, and more knowledgeable than our men. If they really want to be the mothers of this nation, this is the way. (Atatürk 1952, 85–86)

In addition to being a responsible mother of the Kemalist era, the "new woman" was also crafted through a process of producing distance. She was distant from the traditional woman, who was scripted as uneducated, unenlightened, and without the opportunity to achieve advancement. She became the sign and visual symbol of the break with the past, a symbolism that Mustafa Kemal himself not only promoted but circulated. He did so personally in his public tours through the inclusion of his wife, a woman who was known and advertised as educated, Westernized, and aligned with the goals of nationalism. He had his adopted daughters brought up as models of the Kemalist woman; one became a professor of history at the newly founded university in Ankara, while the other (Sabiha Gökçen) became the first military aviator in Turkey and, incidently, was involved in bombing rebels in the Kurdish rebellion.[8] As Arat states:

The image of Sabiha Gökçen in her air force uniform with respectful male onlookers, including her proud father, is ingrained in the collective consciousness of at least the educated urbanites in Turkey. Figuratively, if the project of modernity aimed for a Westernizing polity that was liberal, democratic, and secular, then a female aviator could herald all. This was a new image for Turkey, a new role model for the country's women. A female military aviator insinuated nationalism (because the Turkish nationalist myth upheld male–female equality), democratic participation of women in the making of the new polity, and a secular ethos (because the Muslim opposition did not promote public activism of women). Turkey was taking wings to the future, with women playing leading roles. (Y. Arat 1997, 98–99)

Furthermore, Kemal's broader endorsement of women's new visibility was attested to by photographs of the period ranging from ballroom dancing to official ceremonies. Photographic images of women were too often exploited for their ideological outcomes. Even the leaders of the Republic attempted to define the meaning of a modern woman by appearing in public in the company of unveiled women (N. Arat 1996, 400). As Göle (1996, 14) states, "photographs of women unveiled, of women in athletic competitions, of female pilots and professionals, and photographs of men and women 'miming' European lifestyles depicted the new modernist interpretations of a 'prestigious' life in the Turkish nation-state." Thus, various parts of Turkey witnessed the circulation of signs and symbols of the modern woman so that everyone could learn their appropriate meanings: the category of woman had been recoded and imagined differently.

Nation and Family

Nations are frequently figured through the iconography of familial and domestic space. The term "nation" derives from *natio*: to be born. We speak of nations as "motherlands" and "fatherlands." Foreigners "adopt" countries that are not their native homes and are naturalized into the national "family." We talk of the "family of nations," of "homelands" and "native."

—A. McClintock, "No Longer in a Future Heaven" (1997, 90–91)

Many writers of nationalism have noted the propensity of nation-builders to equate the nation to family (e.g., Cockburn 1998; McClintock 1997; Nagel 1998). Yuval-Davis (1993) reminds us that in France, it was *La Patrie*, a figure of a woman giving birth that personified the revolution. In South Africa, Gaiskell and Unterhaulter suggest that Afrikaner women appear regularly in the rhetoric and imagery of the Afrikaner "volk" (people), and that "they have figured overwhelmingly as mothers" (1989, 60). Nationalists in Muslim Afghanistan conceive resource control (particularly labor, property, and women) as a matter of honor. With honor linked to the observance of purdah, this practice became viewed as a key element in the protection of a family's pride and honor (see Nagel 1998). As we learn from these and other studies, there is a relationship between nation and family in a variety of contexts that range from issues of reproduction and sexuality to fashion. Similar parallels can be observed in the context of Turkey, especially in the way in which nation-building became involved in a generalized longing for a different way of life and images of family became entangled in this longing.

The scripting of the "new woman" of the Kemalist era concerned not only her distance from the past and her ties to the future, but also her credentials, which were to be earned in the new modern family. On 17 February 1926, major changes in the life of Turkish women were introduced by the adoption of the Swiss Civil Code in place of the Islamic Family Code of Turkey. This new, secular civil code introduced civil marriage and divorce. Polygamy was abolished and monogamy was normalized. Divorce was no longer the sole prerogative of men. Gendered inheritance practices gave way to equal rights of inheritance. The first, minimum-age requirement for marriage was determined by law at seventeen for women and eighteen for men. Marriage by representation was abolished and replaced with the principle of civil, legal marriage with the common consent of both groom and bride (see Taşkiran 1976, 71–72). The new, secular family code was meant to change the very structure of Turkish domestic life and bring it closer to models of nuclear family known in Western Europe (Starr 1989, 498). Criticism of this new code was prohibited by law. However, one newspaper published a cartoon depicting the new "emancipated" Turkish woman stepping onto the dirigible of "liberation" and releasing weights of honor, shame, and virtue in order to lift off. The owner, the editor, and the cartoonist were arrested on charges of inciting revolt (Kocturk 1992, 31). Other similar incidences took place, and a new press law, introduced in 1931, gave the nation-state the right to close down newspapers and magazines for publishing anything that conflicted with its general policies (see Keyder 1987, 99).

Not only did Kemalist reformers attempt to transform family life and grant women new rights under Turkey's new, secular civil law (such as the right to choose their own spouses, initiate divorce, and demand child custody [see Z. Arat 1994, 57]), but even Anatolian peasant women were invoked as figures in the route toward change. The attributes of Anatolian peasant women, who were noted for their participation in the War of National Independence and their dedication to their families, were accentuated in the following discourse of Mustafa Kemal:

The Anatolian woman has her part in these sublime acts of self-sacrifice and must be remembered with gratitude, by each one of us. Nowhere in the world has there been a more intensive effort than the one made by the Anatolian peasant women. Woman was the source of a vital dynamism: who ploughed the fields? She did. Who sowed the grain? She. Who turned into a woodcutter and wielded the axe? She did. Who kept the fires of home burning. She. Who, notwithstanding rain or wind, heat or cold, carried the ammunition to the front. She did, again and again.
    The Anatolian woman is divine in her devotion.
    Let us therefore honor this courageous and self-sacrificing woman. It is for us to pledge ourselves to accept woman as our partner in all our social work, to live with her, to make her our companion in the scientific, moral, social and economic realm. I believe that is the road to follow. (cited in Yeğenoğlu 1998, 135)

Anatolian women were visibly targeted as both the "savers" and the "saved" ones: they would save the Republican movement from "degeneration," while these reforms in turn saved them from the fanaticism of Islam. In this way, the "true" Kemalist woman was to serve as a bridge between civilization and nation (Göle 1996, 64).

However, it is worth mentioning here that early anthropological and sociological studies in Turkey (e.g., Stirling 1965) documented that rural peasant women were largely unaffected by these secular codes, as past customs and practices still tended to dominate their marriage, inheritance, and property relations. My own work in contemporary northwestern Turkey shows that polygamy is still practiced by rural, large-landowning classes; rural men and women still engage in arranged marriages at young ages; property inheritance is still overwhelmingly gendered; educational attainment is much lower among females than males (see Ilcan 1994, 1996a); and women's right to vote in local village elections is still strongly influenced by kin relations and class-based interest groups. In this regional setting, it was only after World War II that the rural populations experienced massive transformations, both economically and culturally. Processes of rural–urban migration, new patterns of social mobility, and notions of nationalism and dress confronted the rural populace (see chapter 5).

REDRESSING THE NATION: DIMENSIONS OF A NEW VISUAL CULTURE

As I have discussed earlier, in the early modernization era in Turkey there was a forceful attempt to eradicate those monuments, figures, and practices that were associated with Ottoman society. To become "civilized" meant that "local culture" had to be abandoned to history, or at least the monuments of the Ottoman period had to be displaced from the center to the archive of the rural interior and behind the modern veil. The nationalization of cultural expression was wrought through the deployment of a semio-visual strategy that attempted to recode and reorder relations in the cultural field. From the perspective of Kemalist reformers, if one could associate in people's minds the idea of religious law, religious education, Islamic time, and Ottoman fashion with the idea of disadvantage (i.e., stagnation, backwardness, etc.), the old habits would cease to be valuable. For modernization to take place and to be effective, the perceived objects associated with it ought to be presented everywhere. This was most effectively achieved through the privileging of "sight" (see Jenks 1995, 2); that is, the Kemalist modernity project would have to be seen to be effective. People were placed into particular coordinates of control, where certain groups (such as "rural educators") and newly developed institutions (such as the People's Houses) would be "seen" as the key figures or sites in spreading nationalism. Also, the attributes of specific groups, such as "modern men" and "modern women," would be seen as the visual markers of the nation-state. The early modernization regime involved a pronounced, public investment in particular groups for the purpose of giving them a new visibility and a new sense of belonging both in the eyes of the nation and in the eyes of the international community.

Modern nations, like Turkey, are products of a nationalism that attempted to establish a mass appeal for new political values, gender identities, and ways of life that differentiated the past from the present and the future. As a social movement geared toward massive and rapid change, nationalism consists of programs of unification and homogeneity and of plans to establish a particular kind of "civilized," populated territory. But as Bauman suggests, the "civilizing process" linked to nationalism involves relations of power, knowledge, and authority between the elite and the masses. As he claims:

Nationalism was, sociologically, an attempt made by the modern elites to recapture the allegiance . . . of the "masses" produced by the early modern transformations and particularly by the cultural rupture between the elites and the rest of the population by the "civilizing process," whose substance was the self-constitution and the self-separation of new elites legitimizing their status by reference to superior culture and knowledge. In the same way in which the modern state needed nationalism for the "primitive accumulation" of authority, nationalism needed coercive powers of the state to promote the postulated dissolution of communal identities in the uniform identity of the nation. (1992, 675)

In addition to the notion that nationalism carries with it a pronounced set of class-based, power/knowledge relations used to create a uniform identity of the nation, nationalism also involves a process in which sight or visuality becomes privileged as a national form of knowing. This linkage between seeing and knowing is especially reinforced when nation-building efforts encourage people to participate in planned, public celebrations of national leaders, national days, and national festivities, to honor national flags and monuments, and to become part of those new environments built to symbolize a new order and future way of life. In the case of Turkey today, there exists a wide variety of Atatürk iconography: busts, statutes, portraits, and excerpts from his speeches have come to exist in numerous public stores, offices, and institutions throughout the country and in a variety of city, town, and rural homes. Even some of the names of boulevards, streets, city squares, and residential quarters are commemorative of Atatürk. Also, one of the most grand monuments within Turkey today, the Mausoleum of Atatürk, which was designed by Turkish architects and constructed between 1944 and 1953, occupies an area of fifteen thousand square meters in Turkey's capital city, Ankara (Erdentuğ and Burçak 1998; Salt 1995).

National Spirits and New Houses

The proliferation of images during and after the emergence of the Western, institutional changes of Kemalism and their related nationalist principles may be seen to constitute dimensions of a "national visual culture." The built environment was one of many sites that needed to be redressed, as it was considered important for the general public to "see" their new nation-state as a home that was distinct from, and that no longer belonged to, the Ottoman past. The development of a modern architecture was one way to accomplish this goal. Bozdoğan informs us that the emergence of a new architecture, called *yeni mimari*, effectively legitimized the architect as a cultural leader, an agent of civilization, with a passionate sense of mission to dissociate the Republic from an Ottoman and Islamic past. This modern architecture of prismatic or cubic forms reinforced, according to Bozdoğan, concrete building construction, wide terraces, cantilevers, and flat roofs. This new architecture symbolized the country's emergence from "Oriental malaise" and its willingness to participate in "contemporary civilization." But, due to the impoverished nature of the Turkish construction industry in the 1930s, a substantial program of housing, urbanism, and rationalized production never materialized. Later, there was a rejection of cubic forms on the grounds that they imposed blankness, and there was movement toward forms inspired by traditional Turkish houses (detached villas and row-houses) discovered in Europe by the prominent architect Sedad Hakki Eldem (Bozdoğan 1997, 137–138). These new architectural developments were, however, only one dimension symbolizing national visual culture.

There were other "houses" that needed to be constituted in the built environment and would, in turn, serve the interests of nation-building by making people conscious of nationalism and its values. Following the Third Congress of the Republican People's Party in 1931, fourteen People's Houses (*Halkevleri*) were established in various cities and towns in Turkey. As Öztürkmen argues, these houses worked to mediate the ideas and images promoted by the new nation-state; to provide a regular flow of information to central institutions for the realization of particular Republican projects (such as the Turkish Language Society [TDK] and the Turkish History Society [TTK], which were set up to provide intelligence in support of the new regime's vision of Turkish nationalism); and to direct control over social and cultural activities. People's Houses also played an important role in the introduction of many novel social activities, such as ballroom dancing, and in the initiation of new political rituals, such as the welcoming of bureaucrats and the celebration of national days. The activities undertaken in the People's Houses were divided into nine categories: language, history, and literature; fine arts; theater; sports; social assistance; public classes and courses; library and publishing; village development; and museums and exhibitions. Each category of activities was designed to support the newly introduced practices of the Republican regime (Öztürkmen 1994, 160–161). Öztürkmen also elaborates on some of these activities:

The "Language and Literature" section . . . pursued studies on modern Turkish, its grammar and literature; organized commemoration days for Turkish intellectuals, artists and heroes; and published the results of such studies in their periodicals. The "Fine Arts" section played an important role in mediating the Republic's image of a contemporary society, forming new choral ensembles and orchestras in the western style, offering musical training and organizing painting and photography exhibitions and competitions. Similarly, the "Theater" section claimed among its new duties the organization of drama courses, the training of public speakers, emphasis on women's roles in theatrical pieces, the promotion of domestic arts and support for the art of the cinema. The "Social Help" section would operate as a charity association, raising funds to help the poor, finding jobs for the unemployed, assisting prisoners, and establishing medical polyclinics. As for the "Village Development" section, it would establish "cordial relations" between village and the city, "embellish" the villages, solve the villagers' problems, and raise their standards of living. The "Public Classes and Courses" section was responsible for running literacy courses, stimulating interest in science, opening laboratories and supporting folk art as a potential job-creating sector. And finally, the "Library" section was entrusted with the tasks of arranging book exhibitions and publicizing new publications. (1994, 164)

The wide array of public activities associated with the People's Houses were not just pedagogical in content: they created and marketed the national spirit throughout the year. Times were set aside for commemorating aspects of national history. These included days that marked the foundation of the Great National Assembly, the defeat of the Greek army, and the proclamation of the Republic as well as festive events that publicized various practices, such as Language Day, Land Day, and the Sports Festival. Additionally, writings on nationalism, reform, and secularism frequently appeared in various People's Houses' journals (such as *Ülkü*), wherein readers were encouraged to "love the flag," to buy domestic products, to be critical of "arranged marriages," and to recognize the "national assets" offered to both domestic and foreign tourists (Öztürkmen 1994, 165–169). Overall, the People's Houses circulated the state's imagination of nation and nationalism, and played a critical role in creating the notion of the nation as a new home.

Circulating New Habits

In *Nationalist Thought and the Colonial World*, Chatterjee (1986) alerts us to a discussion of Indian nationalist discourses of home. He suggests that when home, and by extension women, are regarded as the principal site for expressing the nation's culture, controversies about a woman's dress, manners, food, education, and her role inside and outside the home become intensified. Similar controversies about women's "national" appearance took place in Turkey too, alongside the concern with men's head-dresses.

In addition to the legal reforms on the status of women within families, there were attempts to dismantle the Ottoman-style dress and appearance. As Kandiyoti points out, "In the Ottoman empire, rank, origin, and ethnicity could be read clearly in the costumes and even the colours that subject populations were allowed to wear. Similarly, men of religion could be clearly distinguished by their turbans and garments" (1997, 122). Attending to physical appearance was relevant to a movement dedicated to advertising itself as a modern nation-state. Particular body images therefore needed to be forged in order to circulate the meaning of a secular nation-state to the masses. Underlining the "universal" characteristics and "international" character of Western clothes, there emerged extensive concern over the "religious and traditional" significance attributed to the *fez*—the red felt cap that was the Ottoman male's traditional headgear—and later to the *çarşaf* (veil).[9] In fact, the scripting of the "modern man" was crafted along the lines of his bodily presentation. The bodies of men, their distribution and habits, could neither go unchanged nor go unnoticed. Their looks were appropriated as a book of instruction, a lesson to be learned, and in this book the *fez* was the archetypal symbol of Ottoman conservatism. In 1925, for the first time, Mustafa Kemal wore a Panama hat in Kastamonu, in the heartland of Islamic conservatism. He declared to a large crowd:

The Turkish people, who founded the Turkish Republic are civilized; they are civilized in history and reality. But I tell you that . . . the people of the Turkish Republic, who claim to be civilized, must prove themselves to be civilized, by their ideas and mentality, by their family life and their way of living. . . . They must prove in fact that they are civilized and advanced persons in their outward aspect also. I shall put my explanation to you in the form of a question:

Is our dress national? (cries of no)

Is it civilized and international? . . . (cries of no, no)

I agree with you. This grotesque mixture of styles is neither national nor international. A civilized international dress is worthy and appropriate for our nation, and we will wear it. Boots and shoes on our feet, trousers on our legs, shirt and tie, jacket and waistcoat—and of course, to complete these, a cover with a brim on our heads. I want to make this clear. This head covering is called a HAT. (cited in Wheatcroft 1995, 208)

In keeping with the reformist ideology, the slogan of radical Kemalists during these early years was "Let's smash the Idols." In 1925 a special "hat law" was introduced. All male Turks were compelled to abandon the *fez* and wear in its place a hat with a brim, thereby ending the system of social and religious distinctions broadcast by a person's headgear (Ahmad 1993, 79). As Göle (1996, 61) suggests, this new code was assumed to convey significant importance for Turkey and was introduced into society as a visual symbol of Westernization.

There was, however, substantial opposition to the hat reform. The one way to control the opponents of the hat reform was to make their offenses, such as wearing the *fez*, punishable in public. Punitive measures were put in place by military authorities so that when the *fez* was banned, seventy-five hundred people were arrested, hundreds were jailed, and over six hundred were executed and hanged in public squares because of their opposition to the hat law (see Zurcher 1993, 181; Keyder 1987, 84). These measures attempted to make everyone aware of the seriousness of not accepting the signs of modern attire and the new "modern man." Consequently, the idea of the *fez* soon came to arouse the sign of the punishment. Yet some groups found the hat reform difficult because the hat's brim interfered with the Muslim prayer posture of prostration, which required touching the forehead to the floor. Since the prayer skullcap had been prohibited along with the *fez*, and since Muslim practice requires that the head be covered during prayer, some Turkish men accommodated themselves to the new law by wearing visored caps and, during prayer, by turning the visors of their new caps to the backs of their heads (Olson 1985, 165). The visor cap became a mobile symbol: it could be worn to meet both the requirements of nationalism and the conventions of Muslim prayer.

In *Portrait of a Turkish Family* Turkish novelist Irfan Orga (1988), illustrates his memories of wearing the *fez* and then the new hat in 1925. He draws our attention to how the hat law was viewed, manipulated, and

resisted by local townspeople. These actions reflected the tensions associated with belonging to a new home. One passage in the novel is most
striking:

When I used to pass through Bayazit all the old men in the coffee-houses and those
sitting at the tables in the streets would look at the cap with the apology of a peak
and shake their grey heads. . . . The men indignantly refused to throw away the fez
and it became a usual sight to see fighting taking place between the supporters of
the new order and the die-hards of the old. Government officials were the first to
give way to Atatürk. They were forced into this position by reason of their work
and the streets became full of bowler hats worn with a self-conscious air. The
children used to throw stones after them and the police arrested men who still
persisted in wearing the fez, the street sellers in desperation put fancy paper hats
on their heads and added a note of unusual gaiety to the market-places. And out
in the country places and the villages the men even wore women's hats in order to
evade arrest. The old men took to tying handkerchiefs on their heads, placing the
offending Christian hat over this, but the police became wise to this ruse and
promptly arrested them. Arrested men were hauled to the police stations in such
great numbers that they could not be dealt with and the white handkerchiefs were
pulled off the bald pates, the insulting head-gear being firmly clamped over the
naked, uneasy heads. (1988, 222–223)

Kemalist reformers, in deserting Ottoman identity by welcoming the hat,
also sought to leave the practice of veiling behind (Göle 1996, 61), a practice that was thought to place Turkey on the side of the East rather than
the West. At the time of the formation of the Republic, the majority of
Turkish women, whether Muslim, Christian, or Jewish, still wore head
coverings of various types (Olson 1985, 164). In an effort to revolutionize
the appearance of Turkish women, Mustafa Kemal gave several speeches
on the need for changes in the styles of clothing worn by women. He was
also willing to tirade crowds against the practice of veiling. In 1929, in an
effort to launch a frontal attack against some Islamic groups that were not
in favor of the public visibility of women, the Kemalist reformers organized
a "Miss Turkey" contest for the first time. The press gave the event great
publicity in the national newspaper, *Cumhuriyet* (Ahmad 1993, 88), in
news articles, and on the covers of magazines. This was only one of the
many semio-visual strategies used to promote the new image of the "modern woman." For example, there was the portrayal of uncovered women
as professionals, pilots, opera singers, and the like (see Zurcher 1993, 196).
More importantly, however, these recoding efforts gave rise to internal
contradictions in that modern women became viewed both as the bearers
of nationalism and as objects of a new standard of beauty (cf. Gelvin 1998,
147–149).

In 1935 a ban on veiling was proposed, but no legal action was taken
despite Mustafa Kemal's contention that the practice was uncivilized. In

some municipalities, however, there were orders against women's traditional clothing. Many incidents were cited of soldiers forcibly removing the veils of women, although there is little evidence of the extent to which these events occurred (Baykan 1992, 142). In northwestern Turkey, rural residents have told me stories of women in townships being forced to remove their veils by military officials during the 1930s. They emphasized how these incidents actually prevented women from traveling to town markets due to their husbands' insistence that they remain covered. In this context, the attempts to change women's appearance had the effect of restricting their spatial movements and of confining their economic and social activities to their home-based environments (see chapter 6). A small change in appearance, such as the removal of the veil, had a great impact on rural women's lives. On a broader scale, those who did not comply with the change were considered distinct from those urban and more educated women who did; they were marked not only as traditional and religious, but also as interfering in the goals of nationalism.

From the perspective of the reformers, women's physical appearance was also thought to be tied to gender segregation: veiling inhibited women's movement. Discussions of veiled women prior to and around the time of the Kemalist reform movement, positioned women in a geography of constraint. Tezer Taşkiran, a feminist and a resolute supporter of the Kemalist movement, emphasized that veiled women in the early twentieth century sat separated from men on the railways, in trams, and on ferryboats, that a married couple was unable to sit together because the sections in public transportation were partitioned with curtains or wooden screens, and that when a husband and wife visited close friends in their home, the men sat and talked in one room and the women in another (1976, 46). These kinds of images of women were also alluded to in a speech delivered by Mustafa Kemal in Izmir in 1923:

In our towns and cities foreigners' attention focuses on the way our women cover themselves. Such observations lead them to assume that our women don't see anything. However, covering, that is required by the religion, to be stated briefly, should be in a simple form which would not be a burden for women and disturb decency. Covering should not be in a form that would isolate a woman from her life and existence. (Atatürk 1952, 217)

In another speech two years later, he emphasized the interrelationship between veiling and incivility and called for a change in women's appearance. As he proclaimed:

Sometimes, in some places, I see women covering their faces with their head scarves or turning their backs when a man approaches. How would you explain such behaviour? Do you really think that the mothers and daughters of a civilized nation would behave so oddly or be so backward? This sort of thinking makes us a laughing-stock in the eyes of foreigners and it must be stopped in the very near future. (cited in Taşkiran 1976, 62)

More significant than linking the veil to gender segregation was that veiling practices would be negatively viewed by the Western world. Changing such traditional images had long been on the reform agenda, since harems, the wearing of veils and the *fez*, and gender segregation were the stereotypical features of Ottoman lifestyles described by the European West. However, no policies were adopted to alter the situation of women's veiling practices (Z. Arat 1994, 63). Overall, in their attempts to modernize women and men, members of the reform movement had taken the Western image of Turkey as "other" and remodeled it by turning their own populace into strangers.

Kemalist nationalism is synonymous with the reform movements known as modernization. To be modern, or to be considered modern by others, meant undertaking a forced migration from an Ottoman-style political economy and Ottoman-inspired cultural practice. This movement was motivated by a highly stylized image of a modern, Western-style nation-state and the cultural depreciation of the home and settled ways that people would be forced to leave. To move and resettle an entire country is a massive undertaking. A major feature of this migration to modernity is the heavy expenditure of "symbolic capital," no less than "symbolic violence" (Bourdieu 1993), in establishing not only the legitimacy of this move, but also the rules, signs, and symbols that would be the currency of transport and the means used to demarcate the path that the migrants should take.

The Kemalist movement was a major settlement practice. It involved the dimensions of both unsettling and resettling a population. It had as its primary aim the unsettling of traditional practices and the displacement of central cultural representations in the passage from an empire to a nation. The movement assigned new codes, signs, and symbols to those that it carried along in its transit, and it was important that no one, excepting those recalcitrant few who engaged in acts of symbolic resistance, be left behind. The movement applied indiscriminately to everyone.

To separate the public from its home and its lifestyle practices meant separating religion from the state to enhance its mobility, and adopting new linguistic systems, regimes of time, and dress codes for the journey to the modern world. The establishment of universal codes of conduct, however, required a new pedagogical style and a way of circulating the signs of modernity to the masses and the West. The Kemalist modernity project would have to be "seen" to be effective. Gender was one of the central instruments in bringing about a newly coded Turkish nation-state. The Turkish modernity project scripted and conscripted two new characters for the transition: the modern woman and the modern man. The former would span the gulf between the past and the future. She was distanced from the past but projected into the future through her recognition in the development of new family codes, particularly through the adoption of the Swiss Civil Code. In contrast, the new modern man was scripted along the lines of his bodily presentation. The bodies of men were a lesson in manners for the Turkish peoples and their neighbors.

In my attempt to understand nation-building and nationalism in the early modern period of Turkey, I have shown that these efforts merged with other forms of imagining community, other mechanisms for positioning citizens, other bases of belonging. The first part of the discussion outlined the plans, aims, and strategies of the modernist project during the early years of the Kemalist reform movement. Here I highlighted the reform efforts as geared toward creating an image of Turkey as a nation-state characterized by the widespread adoption of a Western system of relations. The second part of my discussion focused on the practical application of the modernity project, its semio-visual technologies, its effects, and its limitations and contradictions. As I have shown, this project was not as seamless and inevitable as it has sometimes been portrayed by other researchers. It ran up against resistance (resistance to the adoption of the Swiss Civil Code, to the hat reform, and to the new visuality of women) and in some ways reproduced the very things that the movement itself was attempting to leave behind. The changes brought about through the Kemalist reform movement hinged on traversing, at infinite speed, the distance and difference between Turkey as an empire and modern nation. The movement of displacing and replacing both a population and its territory relied heavily on the symbolic resources it was able to mobilize for the passage. While the violence of this migration to modernity is, by and large, of a different order than that experienced by other diasporic groups in terms of the means used in forced exiles and expulsions, the Turkish nation-building movement nevertheless stands as another example of the many massive cultural movements witnessed in the twentieth century.

NOTES

1. In 1934, Mustafa Kemal adopted the name Atatürk, embodying his station as father/ancestor of the Turks, and became known as Mustafa Kemal Atatürk.

2. Closely allied to this form of modernity was, among other things, the development of the "modern woman" and the "modern man." Both were the subject and object of social and legal change. The former was considered the bridge between the past and the future, therefore embodying the idea of continuity (cf. McClintock 1997, 92), and the latter was thought to represent the progressive agent of modernity within a secular nation-state.

3. In terms of diversity, Laz, Georgians, Abkhazians, Azeris, Kurds, Turkmen, Yoruks, Circassians, Greeks, Armenians, Albanians, Bosnians, Tatars, and other ethnic and linguistic groups occupied Ottoman territories.

4. However, these efforts were slowed down when the world economic crisis reached Turkey in 1929 and 1930.

5. See Y. Arat (1997) for a discussion of the adoption of Taylorism in housework during the early Republican era in Turkey.

6. See F. Ahmad (1996) for a discussion on "National Schools" and the "script revolution."

7. See Urry (2000a) for a discussion on the relationship between national citizenship and processes of communication.

8. Between 1924 and 1925 a Kurdish rebellion emerged to challenge the new nation-state. This rebellion "put the government back on a war footing, with independence courts enjoying extraordinary powers to repress Kurdish demands in the east, and using them with impunity" (Keyder 1987, 83). However, as part of the move toward establishing an ethnically uniform nation-state, the Kurds living in Turkey suffered systematic repression. Starting in the early formation of the Turkish Republic, a vigorous campaign against the Kurds ensued. Kurdish associations, schools, publications, religious fraternities, and teaching foundations were all banned.

9. In 1829 the turban was replaced by the *fez* as the appropriate headgear for male civilians (see Kesaba 1997, 24–25). Toward the end of the nineteenth century women began to wear *çarşaf*s in place of *ferace*s when they were in public. These *çarşaf*s were worn up to the Republican period. The most conservative one was a full skirt with a pelerine that hung down in the back and covered the head. It was black and the face was obscured by a black veil (Taşkiran 1976, 47).

CHAPTER 3

ETHNOGRAPHIC TRANSITS

Like many citizens in the West, I was brought up to believe that mobility is a normal feature of modernity and that attaining distance not only is a modern directive, but also provides a modern sense of perspective. Yet it has been my experience that being either at home or away brings its own set of challenges; that micro and macro movements can bring political and social hardship in addition to any economic benefit that may be gained; and that distance creates its own set of tensions and can be quite deceptive. Recollecting my many travels from Canada to Turkey as a child, my school years living in Germany as both a resident outsider and a tourist, and my journeys as a graduate student and academic researcher to urban and rural places in North America and Europe, has made me sensitive to the practice of movement. Movement constrains and enables the formation of relationships. It brings with it a sense of loss of both the expectations and the possibilities that come from belonging with people and to places while opening up new possibilities as well as shaping new vulnerabilities, since one may no longer know what to expect or what is expected. These mobile practices have led me to reflect on the sensibilities of movement and the longing associated with belonging.

In this chapter, I inquire into categories that are so often taken for granted and the ways in which movement, location, and displacement are woven into studies of cultural production that form the making of ethnography. This inquiry is influenced by the insights and ideas pertaining to contemporary ethnography (e.g., Gupta 1999; Stewart 1996; Phillips 1996; Appadurai 1996; Cole 1995; Abu-Lughod 1993). It is also based on my ethnographic experiences of working and living with people in another cultural milieu.

A wide array of ethnographic accounts as well as distinct and varied questions of movement have emerged within global and local fields of study. Here I refer to the research on the historical development of industrialization in the West and in other regions across the globe; the rise of nationalism and its ideologies; the mass migrations of peoples and lifestyles from one home to another; the transformation of values and outlooks as a consequence of planned economic development; and the ways in which ordinary people deploy mobility in the practice of their everyday lives. Such thematic fields of study embody dimensions of movement and place and have encouraged me to inquire into the nature of these relations.

Movement not only refers to the movement of peoples but to the construction of categories, ideas, and practices of mobility in diverse fields. I think about the variety of ethnographic experiences connected to relations of "habitation" in various ethnographic "fields" of knowledge, practice, and imagination, such as communities, immigrant neighborhoods, inner-city ghettos, town squares, museum exhibitions, regions, archives, schools, churches, beaches, shopping malls, common or elite institutions, and so on. The dynamics of entering, leaving, and relating in such fields make me think about the various mobile practices entailed in ethnography. Similarly, the practices of writing, listening, retelling, translating, or rereading ethnographic insights reflect various mobile, transitional, and transformative dimensions of doing ethnographic research. As a consequence, I find myself drawn to the concepts, styles, and cultural dimensions of ethnographic movements.

In my own research and writing, the concept of movement leads me to focus on the changing history of locations and the transformation of social relations in particular spaces and times; the range of displacements that have come to characterize people's lives, including the lives of ethnographers; and the wide realm of habitation practices that have mobile elements attached to them. Whether studying the cultural and political dimensions of a "community" or conducting archival research in a United Nations library—two fields that I have entered—we not only have to travel, we also have to partake in various other practices and processes of displacement. These processes range from the inclusion or exclusion of particular ethnographic strategies, to the incorporation or the collaboration of others in the research process, to the transfiguration of ethnographic information, to the repeated visiting of peoples, places, or documents. Along with the political and social conditions that shape these comings and goings for researchers, travels within and outside such variable fields provide a basis for understanding how spatial and temporal practices generate knowledges, stories, imaginations, and other collective productions. To this should be added the appropriation, translation, or displacement of knowledge that occurs in the processes of writing ethnography. Movements of all sorts are actively created, negotiated, and renegotiated through relations that circumscribe ethnographic practices in a variety of contingent environments. Within this context, I suggest that these mobile dimensions alert our senses and our sensibilities to a style of research that does not focus on one place or location, whether of peoples, places, or cultures; instead, they interact within many conventional and unconventional fields and open up multiple displacements, rather than "placements," of inquiry. The ethnographic practices—of writing against culture (Abu-Lughod 1993), writing against writing culture (Cole 1995), listening and translating (Phillips 1996), remembering and retelling (Stewart 1996), and resisting views of culture as a "noun" (Appadurai 1996)—are social activities that involve both transformation and movement. I understand movement not in relative terms, in the way that practices of ethnography move from point to point in a contained field, but in terms of how the practice of ethnography moves through a multiplicity of ethnographic fields and insights.

ETHNOGRAPHIC SURROUNDINGS

> Culture . . . is a space of imagination, critique, and desire produced in and through mediating forms. It is not something that can be set "straight" but it has to be tracked through its moves and versions, its sites of encounter and engagement, its pride and regrets, its permeabilities and vulnerabilities, its nervous shifts from one thing to another, its moments of self-possession and dispersal.
> —K. Stewart, *A Space on the Side of the Road* (1996, 9)

I consider my recent work, and what has been produced from it, as ethnographic. The wide array of methods employed to study social and historical aspects of other cultures has led me to reflect on the field-sensitive nature of ethnographic practices and the "field" in which these practices occur. During my graduate studies, I remember participating in university seminar debates about the "particularities" of communities, neighborhoods, and rites of passages in ethnographic accounts of culture. The ethnographies of the "particular"—the stories written by those who spoke in detail of lives and life histories—moved me, and I saw in these accounts the great potential for doing interdisciplinary research. However, the discussions always seemed to come round to the problem of the place of ethnographies in the practice of research and the idea that they belonged to certain theoretical perspectives, to certain academic disciplines, and to specific research fields. As I have always studied in graduate departments that combined anthropology and sociology, the idea that these methods of understanding and analysis should be kept in *their* place seemed ironically out of place. One of my preoccupations (although not clearly formulated at the time of my doctoral research) was to work against a rarefaction of research endeavors that seemed to me to be all too disciplinary in their aim.[1] As I began working between the respective disciplinary webs of both sociology and anthropology, I became intrigued by the differences and similarities among social anthropology, qualitative sociology, and cultural studies (the latter especially in the Birmingham tradition)[2] on issues of field research and its cultural production. Moving in the space between these disciplines and their "informal division of labour" (Barrett 1999, 29), I came to understand the importance of interdisciplinarity and how unsettling this maneuvering practice could be, both to the field of knowledge and to the long-standing canonical features of those settled within their "disciplinary habitus" (Clifford 1997). It was in this circuit of movement, and the challenges it entailed, that I encountered a new field of possibilities beyond the discipline-bound methods.

I am still persuaded by my early views on the advantages of interdisciplinary thought for ethnographic research and writing. In much of my ethnographic research I seek to cross disciplinary boundaries without firmly holding to canonical distinctions around which these boundaries have been organized. In this context, the "particularities" of ethnography—the detailed stories that circulate in the "field," the numerable relations that stretch from place to place, the unimaginable encumbrances that people live with from day to day—could be found everywhere. They reveal themselves within archival information, recorded field notes, remembered events, life histories, and photographs, and through the thoughts generated by other writers on similar matters of interest. These particularities invade and disperse themselves in my writing, in the itinerancy of my questions, connections, and conceptions of social lives and histories. They manifest in the included voices that appear and echo in my text. Like other writers, I find the mixing of different voices and styles of presentation both challenging and productive. In this writing-transforming context, I want others to speak within and interrupt my prose so that the development of ideas becomes a reflexive and collective, rather than a conclusive, process.

The "particularities" of field research return throughout this writing process. The concern for particularities, that is, for the in-depth observations and tales of a site, is not simply an overcommitment on the part of ethnographers to account for profuse aspects of local cultures; it is also a willingness to ensure that the broader aspects of the field, and those issues that traverse local boundaries, are included in the process. As Appadurai warns, "ethnographers can no longer be content with the thickness they bring to the local and the particular, nor can they assume that as they approach the local, they approach something more elementary, more contingent, and thus more real than life seen in larger-scale perspectives" (1996, 54). He suggests that what is locally significant has transnational implications somewhere. Social lives are tied to images, ideas, and opportunities that come from elsewhere and are often mediated by large-scale realities, such as those of mass media and communications as well as mass-mediated narratives. This focus complements Clifford's concern with those "old localizing strategies" that aim to focus our attention on bounded communities, organic cultures, or fixed regions. These strategies, according to Clifford, are unable to account for the transcultural circuits of populations, cultures, and capital. Like Appadurai, he is more interested in the ways in which "diasporic dimensions" create ties between people in diverse locations or deconstruct the essentialist constructions of modernity (Clifford 1994). Perhaps more significantly, both authors echo their loss of confidence in "place" as an epistemological ordering principle in cultural or ethnographic productions (see also Gupta 1999; Marcus 1989).

There is no doubt that critical concerns emerge when delineating the thickness of the local at the expense of ignoring its contextual belongings. However, for me, no region, place, population, territory, human settlement, or even nation-state is ever completely bounded: there are always openings and developments that bring about change in any given location. The local interfaces with other broader processes. Here I think about a geographic region of Turkey now referred to as Central Turkey—but historically known as Anatolia or Asia Minor—and believed to be one of the oldest human settlements, dating back to the eighth millennium B.C. As with other regions inside and outside Turkey, this region has been unsettled by the circulation of peoples, practices, and materials of the past several centuries. It is not a region legible, visible, autonomous, or readable in its entirety. It has been distinguished by a mixture of Asian and Western cultures and by the broad influence of a variety of cultural dimensions that range from the early settlement practices of Hittite peoples who spoke an Indo-European language, to the political and cultural influences of the Eastern Roman Empire, to the later development of Greek Orthodox Christian cultures. Infilled with social differences and divisions, this region becomes a diasporic assemblage open to broader perspectives of cultural production. In this regard, a region or a place is the "ongoing matrix and record of social processes" which are themselves not merely local but exist at numerous scales (Shields 1999, 308).

Broadening the parameters of locality has always entailed the risk of transforming sites into panoramas or locations of geographical infinitude. Various strategies of generalization have been involved in such enlarging endeavors, including analogical reasoning, cross-cultural comparison, and standardization. For example, I think of the ways in which government bodies and international organizations, such as the United Nations, have classified and immobilized generations of individuals who, by virtue of their birth, residence, or lineage, do not fit neatly into any ready-made economic or statistical class. Such standardization strategies lock populations into places and sets of global relations wherein they do see themselves as belonging, thus discounting their differences, struggles, and the ways in which local spaces and practices regulate, influence, or transform other segments of populations (see Ilcan and Phillips 2000 on the global mapping of populations). These globalizing strategies raise questions about the politics of inclusion and exclusion in the discourses and practices of "globalization" movements.

In the attempt to move beyond the limitations of both globalizing strategies and small-scale or "microethnography" (Ifekwunigwe 1999; Wolcott 1995), contemporary feminist ethnographers, and those working in the emerging "new ethnography," seek to consider the various ways in which the local and the global articulate and are articulated. For me, the issues related to ethnography's local features are of critical concern when the local and the global are treated separately from one another, that is, when cultural dimensions of place are generalized to the point wherein local cultural forms are supplanted by global views. The globalization of small-scale ethnography tends to overlook the expansion and complexity of people's lived relations in local environments. These global efforts to bound locality and culture may make local lives appear unsophisticated or unconnected to wider social practices and institutions, to the historical or contemporary conflicts of nationalism, to the processes of great technological transformation, or to relations of space and displacement. This is an important part of the justification for what Abu-Lughod (1993) terms "writing against culture."

In *Writing Women's Worlds*, Abu-Lughod alerts us to how ethnographic description can reproduce the methods of "othering" and can traffic in generalizations. For her, generalizations produce the effects of homogenization. They risk smoothing over contradictions and conflicts of interest, and can, as a consequence, contribute to the creation of bounded "cultures." As she states: "In the process of generalizing from experiences and conversations with a number of specific people in a community, the anthropologist may flatten out their differences and homogenize them" (1993, 9). Likewise, in *Culture, Power, Place*, Gupta and Ferguson suggest that speaking of a bounded culture—a separate, individuated cultural entity typically associated with a "people" or a "tribe"—lends itself to a form of generalization, such as that of cross-cultural comparison, that makes it possible to bound the ethnographic object and make wide-ranging claims from a diversity of isolated cases (1999a, 1).

Gupta and Ferguson's concern over the strategies used in cross-cultural comparison, and Abu-Lughod's emphasis on the dangers associated with generalizing and homogenizing dimensions of culture, are critical issues for ethnographic practice. Consider, for example, the ways in which so-called Middle Eastern peoples have been depicted in various ethnographic and media accounts that conjure up images of them and their places of belonging as "other," that depict particular rites of passages as alien, that present women's veiling practices as iconic of the subordination of women,[3] and that depict ways of thinking as stemming from their formal religious discourses and practices. The popularization and homogenization of "cultures" can be easily found in print media, such as travel guides. I recall the "authoritative" travel guides on Turkey that I have purchased over the years, with their colorful depictions of "covered," chubby Turkish women, of mosques overshadowing the exotic city lights, of the crowded, poor-looking neighborhoods, and of the rules that travelers to Turkey should abide by. A contemporary *Let's Go* guide to Greece and Turkey states: "For men, Turkey is probably one of *the* ideal budget travel destinations; some compare it to Greece ten years ago, pre-tourist influx. But the restrictive customs that continue to give women subordinate status (if unofficially) in Turkey mean that the country needs more than a hoped-for EC [European Community] membership to modernize in the Western sense of the word" (1994, 393). Aside from its clearly Western perspective, this statement ignores an understanding of how the history of locations and the locations of history within Turkey (and elsewhere) are marked by the interrelationships of gender, class, and cultural tourism. Similarly, a recent article publicized by *The Economist*, titled "Turkey: Atatürk's Long Shadow" (2000), dwells on Turkey's political, economic, and cultural limitations and calls for a return for the citizens of Turkey to practice Atatürk's founding democratic principles. In this article no attention is given to the manner in which political power inside and outside Turkey is exercised, nor is attention given to the shifting alliances between diverse authorities that govern its economy and cultural practices. Also ignored is the way that Western states and institutions, such as the International Monetary Fund (IMF) and the World Bank, have placed various Turkish sectors and industries within a geopolitical nexus and have been implicated in the country's current economic debt crisis. In these venues, the concept of culture is simply just "this" or "that," and has no mobile or transformative dimensions.

Generalized accounts tend to represent culture as a fixed entity or to treat it as a noun. To resist the noun form of culture, Appadurai suggests "stressing the dimensionality of culture rather than its substantiality [which] permits our thinking of culture less as a property of individuals and groups and more as a heuristic device that we can use to talk about difference" (1996, 13). Departing from the conception of culture as fixed in place and time provides an opportunity for those interested in studying such dimensional qualities to focus on the mobile dimensions of cultural production. In following these movements we may come to recognize the processes of transit and transition, and understand the impact that they have on local and global cultural dimensions (see Phillips and Ilcan 2000). These processes have critical implications for thinking about the dimensional qualities of culture in terms of its openings and passages.

In the context of the emerging new ethnography, Stewart (1996) views the cultural dimensions of the Appalachian coal-mining region of south-western West Virginia as a transportable "nervous system." This nervous system (see Taussig 1992) embodies the wild, political oscillations between one thing and another, where moments of cultural naturalization and de-naturalization interlock, where structures of feelings form, and where its force and its texted politics of desire circulate. This system does not permit a view of culture that hinges on order, unity, tradition, coherence, and singularity; instead, it is both global and local, both tactile and imaginary, both set and fleeting, both one thing and another (Stewart 1996, 20–21). The new ethnography that Stewart imagines involves displacing not just the signs or the projects of essentialism (generalizations, reifications), but also the desire to decontaminate meaning and the arranged ordering of objects and subjects. As she says, this new ethnography would involve an effort to

dwell in the uncertain space of error or gap not just to police the errors and crimes of representation but to imagine the ontology and epistemology of precise cultural practices including our own modes of exegesis and explanation. It would mean displacing the rigid discipline of "subject" and "object" that sets Us apart and leaves Them inert and without agency. It would mean displacing the premature urge to classify, code, contextualize, and name long enough to imagine something of the texture and density of spaces of desire that proliferate in Othered places. (1996, 26)

In line with Stewart's emphasis on how displacement activities form part of the emerging new ethnography, I would like to suggest that the produc-tion of such an ethnography calls for a particular style of learning to do and understand ethnography. This new ethnographer parallels Braidotti's "nomadic polygot" (1994, 15), as one who becomes compassionate about studying the inconsistencies within culture, the conflicts existing between groups and territories of the same culture, the iteration of rhythms of pro-duction and rites of passages, and the arbitrariness of language and ter-minology that a researcher works with. A focus on the inconsistences and the conflicts within and across a particular community, region, or cultural formation opens up different dimensions of culture. This nomadic style of ethnography works toward disengaging the sedentary nature of words, things, or customs, toward unsettling commonsensical meanings, and to-ward deconstructing established forms of "what ought to be," as in the case of "writing culture" and its truth-claims. It also may entail conver-sations, dialogues, and exchanges with other people "in the field" who may be considered marginal—immigrants, migrants, or minorities—but who nevertheless have something to teach us about everyday political affairs, whether these be class- or gender-based or matters of nationalism, region-alism, or ethnicity (see chapters 5 and 6).

In contradistinction to the great many generalizations that have been made about a specific "culture," such as those that form the subject of Said's discussion of Orientalism (1978), a nomadic ethnographic orienta-tion brings to life the fragmentary and tangled dimensions of culture. It expresses the successive shifts and changing coordinates of culture rather than its essential unity. Researching the dimensions of culture becomes for me a process of undoing the stable practices associated with viewing culture as a noun. This process lends itself to opening the boundaries that are created from stereotypical familiarity with one geographic, regional, or lin-guistic site. It necessitates the movement back and forth between the local and the global, and calls for an analytical focus on places and relations of transit and transition.

MOBILE INSIGHTS

> [T]ravelling as a practice of bold omission and minute depiction allows one to (become) shamelessly hybridize(d) as one shuttles back and forth between critical blindness and critical insight.
> —T. Minh-ha, "Other Than Myself/My Other Self" (1994, 24)

For some time now, I have concentrated on the ways in which people's lived experience, especially in regard to those on the margins of dominant society, force us to think again about the nature of the "outside," the for-eign, or the migrant within. This interest has been cultivated through my contact with those social groups (immigrants, guest workers, "gypsies," inmarrying women) who live in worlds that feel alien to them and who experience a sense of loss or separation from a place they identify as home. During one of my lengthy research excursions to the northwestern region of Turkey in the late 1980s, I was conducting research on relations of domination and subordination, with a substantive focus on farm and mi-grant groups. These groups had raised concerns about the expulsion of ethnic Turks from Bulgaria to Turkey in 1989. In a Bulgarian campaign that portrayed ethnic Turks as endangering national "identity" and at-tempted to assimilate this group into Slavic society, thousands of ethnic Turks were compelled to leave their homes in northern and southeastern Bulgaria (see chapter 5). This mass exodus was the predecessor of other coercive migrations that took place during and after the dissolution of po-litical regimes in Europe. By August 1989, some 310,000 ethnic Turks had made their way to Turkey (see Van Hear 1998). Their arrival was heralded in the Turkish media and was widely covered in Turkish television, news-papers, and radio broadcasts, and became a source of great concern for the rural peoples that I was living with in northwestern Turkey. For example, some people feared the loss of their seasonal, migrant jobs to this unemployed population. They were also concerned that they would be forced to support the new immigrants by hiring them as workers on their farms or giving them places to sleep in their homes. This event served to remind me of the diverse meanings attached to "home" and "homeland," the politics that surround practices of settlement and displacement, and the ways in which one can be at home in movement and how movement can be one's home.

My reading of migrant literature has fostered further questions about the relation between home and displacement. This literature tends to emphasize how a difficult, destabilizing present leads to a nostalgia for the past. Emine Sevgi Özdamar, a Turkish-born writer who later emigrated to Germany, illustrates this relation in her book *Mother Tongue*. She offers a compelling exploration of migrancy and the experience of losing one's mother tongue for Turkish guest workers living in Germany. In this novel, the text itself can be read as theater or straight prose. The opening of the novel reads: "In my language, 'tongue' means 'language.' A tongue has no bones: twist it in any direction and it will turn that way" (1994, 9). Throughout the work, we learn about the twists and turns of the mother tongue, of the language that once seemed familiar but became foreign as it mixed with another. We learn about the war of liberation in Turkey during the 1920s when Atatürk outlawed the Arabic script and brought in the Latin script to ally Turkey with its modern neighbors (see chapter 2). We learn about the *gecekondu*s (the Turkish city slum houses that were built overnight to accommodate rural–urban migrants), the movement of workers from Turkey to Germany and the immigration policies that governed them, the living conditions of guest workers in Germany and their longings for home, and the many stories of the *gastarbeiter* and their practices of resistance.

Özdamar's ethnographic account of migrant tales offers readers a moving depiction of the tales of passage and transition, of travels across borders, and of the translation between languages and cultures. Such stories articulate the struggles of the mother tongue. In her words:

I can remember sentences now, sentences [my mother] said in her mother tongue, except that when I imagine her voice, the sentences themselves sound in my ears like a foreign language I know well. When I asked her why Istanbul had become so dark, she said, "Istanbul has always been this dark, it's your eyes that have grown used to *Alamanian* [German] lights." (1994, 9–10)

For me, this novel calls up numerous memories of the *Alamanian* lights and *Alamanian* sites forged during my time in Germany in the early 1970s and the times that I visited my family there in the 1980s. This past life persists in all the particulars of its events localized in time, though it seems that it ought to be concealed by the present, by modernity. Like a thickening whisper, my memories of the past graft themselves onto sites of movements: I remember seeing and feeling a migrant sensibility, a longing in belonging, on the streets and in the air of German cities such as Berlin, Düsseldorf, and Frankfurt. These were sites where some corner stores and apartment windows were marked by dangling Turkish flags; where small coffee shops (run and operated by guest workers) were filled with lively talk and sprightly games of backgammon, and decorated with ornate copper objects from "home"; where planes departed from Frankfurt to Istanbul almost on the hour; and where, in the summer months, the Autobahn transported streams of guest workers and their families back to their "home" towns and villages. I also recollect the xenophobia: the German-owned restaurants that wore a small sign near their doorways that read, "No dogs or Turks allowed"; the ethnic slurs such as *"Türken raus!"* (Turks get out!) painted on walls in Kreuzberg (the Turkish section of Berlin); the German news magazine *Der Spiegal*, which covered stories on issues related to Turkish struggles in Germany; and the *Überfremdungsängste* (fears of overforeignization) that mobilized right-wing movements in Germany at the time.

These recollections foretold of the potential risks confronting some populations, risks that forced them to undertake precautionary measures should the necessity for escape arise. They tell me of the images of migrancy even though many other images are present without being represented or tied to other images such as *Ausländer* (lit., "from outside the country") or *Einwanderer* ("immigrants"). They tell me of the conduct, the coordination, and the inhabitation of movements. They alert me to how my perceptions—impregnated with images of a period of history—are tied to the movements of duration that prolong them, such that the past remains in the present (if only as a potential). My images of migrancy and my recollections of the places they occupy or pass through serve to refresh my mobile sensitivity from time to time.

What then does it mean for a researcher to embody a mobile sensitivity? All ethnographers have a consciousness of sorts. But what interests me is the research that brings dimensions of mobility to the forefront of ethnographic practices. Often feminist and critical, an ethnographer's mobile sensitivity or nomadic awareness consists in an image of a past that lives on in the present and is a record of the activities that elucidate possibilities of relational change that derive from rethinking past events and storied lives. A mobile sensitivity resists dominant ways of representing culture in research and writing. It displaces the horizon of queries that dwell on the rigid polarities of center and periphery and focuses instead on the relations and sites of habitation, transit, and transition. This type of sensitivity lingers in a mode of approaching but never quite arriving, or "a moving toward," as Stewart aptly puts it (1996, 89). It views identity as mobile (Braidotti 1994, 35) and in a process of developing, or in a process of what

Mouffe terms "permanent hybridization and nomadization" (1994, 110). Moreover, this mobile sensitivity can encompass a variety of ethnographic styles and interdisciplinary outlooks. It is a kind of disposition toward practice that is influenced by the positionality of the researchers, the situations they find themselves in, and the subject matters and agencies they investigate.

There is a diversity of provisional, mobile activities that researchers engage in in the making of ethnography. These activities range from the activity of collecting data from local libraries and archival sites; to the compilation and integration of varied forms of knowledge stemming from memories, interviews, conversations, stories, poems, arguments, and life histories; to the exchange of thoughts on life experiences, local and world events, and rites of passages; to the ethnographer's writing about dimensions of culture and the shifts in and circuits of travel that this requires when searching through articles, archival documents, field notes, tape recordings, photographs, and unwritten but remembered conversations; to the ethnographer's recollection of those situations and the very real ideological and social constraints confronted when doing research. In many ways, researchers formulate, transmit, and experience information in a culture of difference and through a manner of connecting, all of which I have found seems to work on the basis of a dispersion in thinking as well as through a focus on transitions and passages without predetermined destinations. Stewart suggests that research is a process of "long dwelling on things re-membered and retold, forgotten and imagined" (1996, 7).

The mobile style of ethnography that I have been describing so far implies the displacement of my place of focus as an ethnographer "in the field." In my ethnographic practices, I pass in between different discursive fields and through diverse spheres of local and global experiences, storytelling, and intellectual inquiry. My encounters in the communities I have lived in and with the people I have come to learn about in Turkey necessitated that I travel in and out of places and people's lives and establish connections and ties in difficult, awkward, and often itinerant circumstances. I remember the dialogues I have had while traveling on buses and trains, on tractors and in taxis; while visiting households teeming with the life of people coming and going; and while experiencing a life of ideas that were developing, merging, and changing. My place of belonging is continually "displaced" as I move from one place to another and create connections through dialogues with others, in writing about others, in thinking through my location and dislocation vis-à-vis other people and other writers. Perhaps this is why I have often felt like a migrant in my research endeavors and why experiences of longing in belonging lead me to unsettle Western rationalities and privilege movement as the organizing principle for studying dimensions of culture.

THE POLITICS OF LOCATION AND DISPLACEMENT

[T]o travel implies movement between fixed positions, a site of departure, a point of arrival, the knowledge of an itinerary. It also intimates
an eventual return, a potential homecoming. Migrancy, on the con-
trary, involves a movement in which neither the points of a departure
nor those of arrival are immutable or certain. It calls for a dwelling in
language, in histories, in identities that are constantly subject to mu-
tation. Always in transit, the promise of a homecoming—completing
the story, domesticating the detour—becomes an impossibility.
                    —I. Chambers, *Migrancy, Culture, Identity* (1994, 5)

My interest in the complexities of movement has been inspired by groups
of people who move through space and time and become entangled in the
politics of location and displacement. I think here of the twentieth-century
*gastarbeiter*s, the migrant workforces imported by European industrial
nations, and the politics of movement linked to them: the large numbers
of people, such as the millions of guest workers living in Western Europe,
who have become displaced from national, regional, or ethnic locations
through processes of resettlement. These processes highlight the politics of
location experienced by migrant workers. On the one hand, these migrant
workers continue to face various forms of oppression and exclusion as a
consequence of their "importedness." Their marginalized status as citizens
or laborers and their belonging to a particular ethnic group engender the
chronic reproduction of disparities and their "otherness" (see chapter 4).
Yet, on the other hand, migrant workers have also been known to challenge
nationalist and racist policies through forms of active protest that bring
about changes in immigration policies, citizenship rights, and employment
and housing opportunities. This example of guest workers, as well as other
collective experiences of displacement in modernity,[4] forces me to think
about the continual emergence of multiple locations and their political
zones, and to develop perspectives on cultural production that can account
for these shifting relations and affiliations.

It is in the midst of labor and population displacements that new concerns over borders, boundaries, identities, and locations arise within anthropology, cultural criticism, and sociology. In *Questions of Travel*,
Kaplan suggests that fixed definitions of locations obscure the shifting relations that occur within and between locations. In her words:

In most theoretical accounts, the influx of immigrants, refugees, and exiles from
the "peripheries" to the metropolitan "centers" both enriches and threatens the
parameters of the nation as well as older cultural identities. Yet definitions of locations as "centers" and "peripheries" only further mystify the divides between
places and people. Centers are not impermeable, stable entities of purely defined
characteristics that come simply to be contaminated or threatened by "others" from

elsewhere. Rather, the large metropoles that draw waves of new populations are dynamic, shifting, complex locations that *exchange* goods, ideas, and culture with many other locations. (1998, 102)

In contemporary times, immigrants, refugees, migrants, and stateless peoples bring to the fore experiences and concerns related to citizenship, borders, identities, and locations (e.g., Urry 2000b; Malkki 1999; Leonard 1999; Jameson and Miyoshi 1999; Lovell 1998; Peck 1995; Kristeva 1991; Anzaldúa 1987). Gupta and Ferguson (1999b) suggest that such concerns are more generally related to diaspora and the mass movements of populations, and to attempts to map the globe as a set of cultural regions (center and periphery, colony and metropole). But these are not the only groups that experience displacement. "For even people remaining in familiar and ancestral places find the nature of the relations to place ineluctably changed and the illusion of a natural and essential connection between place and the culture broken" (Gupta and Ferguson 1999b, 38). It is within this context that I ask: Is there a politics of location and displacement, of movement, that not only underlines migrant populations but shapes ethnographic practices?

In *Modernity at Large*, Appadurai introduces us to the "landscapes of group identity," or what he refers to as "ethnoscape." This term highlights the plights of perspective and representation that ethnographers encounter in the social, territorial, and cultural reproduction of group identity. A notion of movement underscores Appadurai's understanding of both ethnoscape and ethnography. He argues that

as groups migrate, regroup in new locations, reconstruct their histories, and reconfigure their ethnic projects, the *ethno* in ethnography takes on a slippery, nonlocalized quality, to which the descriptive practices of anthropology will have to respond. The landscapes of group identity—the ethnoscapes—around the world are no longer familiar anthropological objects, insofar as groups are no longer tightly territorialized, spatially bounded, historically self conscious or culturally homogeneous. We have fewer cultures in the world and more internal cultural debates. (1996, 48)

One of the most vivid ethnographic examples of migrant groups that come to my mind are rural women living in various regions of Turkey. For centuries these women have been compelled to travel to new locations upon marriage. In these locations they are confronted with new social responsibilities and relations of authority, and are encouraged to make a home for themselves in what is sometimes considered an alien environment. Known as *gelin*, or the "ones who come," these women share a migrant history. At very young ages they are taught to anticipate their eventual migration and to develop a mobile sensitivity that acts as a device for learning to move ahead. They are taught that they will marry and move away from their natal "homeland" and are considered migrants by both of their families. In this way they live the life of the migrant rather than the traveler. Their migrancy may imply that they have a landscape of identity, an ethnoscape, that works to mitigate some of the negative effects of being "outsiders" even at "home." In fact, under some conditions, their collective experiences of displacement have brought them in solidarity with one another and have encouraged them to develop their own particular cultural and political practices of unsettlement (see chapter 6). Their stories, their rememberings, and their longing in belonging enact the density of a lived spatial politics, or what Stewart might call a lived "cultural poetics" (1996).

In *A Space on the Side of the Road: Cultural Poetics in an "Other" America*, Stewart tells readers about the ethnographic stories of a "space on the side of the road," a place in the hardcore Appalachian coal-mining region of southwestern West Virginia. These stories enact the density, texture, and force of a lived cultural poetics somewhere between the real and imagined hinterlands of "America." Her ethnography moves away from cultural productions that constitute this region as frozen into essentialized "objects" and fixed identities. Instead, it highlights local cultures and local voices that are set in motion through a network of tellings and retellings, displacements, rememberings, and pieced-together fragments. In drawing upon the insights of Barthes, Bakhtin, and Benjamin, Stewart offers innovative insights of the local culture of this region by viewing culture as a process "constituted in use and therefore likely to be tense, contradictory, dialectical, dialogic, texted, textured, both practical and imaginary, and infilled with desire" (1996, 5). Like other contemporary ethnographies, Stewart's ethnography speaks to the politics of location and the tellings of displacement in a field that brings to the forefront local assemblages of knowledges.

Questions relating to the politics of location and displacement have permeated contemporary and feminist ethnography, and inspired much research on the anthropology and sociology of place. I have learned from those ethnographers, like Stewart (1996), to be conscious of the politics of positionality and place that circumscribe ethnographic research and writing. A number of other ethnographic productions come to mind here, but I will select only a few that have given me pause for thought. Let me first start with Cole's recent insights into the work of Boasian anthropologist Ruth Landes and her early ethnography of race and gender in Bahia, Brazil. In this work, Cole (1995, 1999) explores Ruth Landes's writing on race, gender, and culture in *City of Women*, an ethnography on women ritual leaders and Afro-Brazilian spirit possession (*candomblé*). In challenging traditional methodological field research practices and subject matter, Landes's ethnography documents the harsh lives of women "for whom the cult houses were havens from marital strife and from daily lives of grinding poverty" (Cole 1999, 23).

Through a temporally sensitive appraisal of Landes's research questions, theoretical frameworks, and writing styles in *City of Women* and in other texts, Cole (1995) argues that Landes's work can be understood as an early example of the practice of "writing against culture." In this context we come to understand how Landes resisted the conventions and methods of "othering" that were becoming popular during the period. The politics of location are borne out in Cole's analysis of Landes's work, especially in terms of how this work is open to broader fields of anthropological knowledge and ethnographic writing styles. Cole provides a rich and insightful analysis of Landes's personal background and work history, and intellectual writings, influences, and relationships (Cole 1995, 1999). Within this analytical field, she identifies the processes by which Landes rejected "ethnographic naturalism," resisted the cataloging of cultural traits, and contested the removal of culture from its social, political, and economic milieu. Landes's research on *candomblé* was informed not only by the 1930s Brazilian context, but also by the nature of U.S. race relations. Landes achieved these various levels of transition by including in her writing personal reflections, stories, and the voices of Bahians. She also gave readers an understanding of the consciousness she had of her positionality as a Jewish woman working in Brazil and the constraints that such a position engendered. These methodological practices were unconventional in anthropology during her day, and her work was labeled as unscientific travelogue and personal memoir. Nevertheless, as Cole argues, Landes's "writing against culture" established race and gender as issues central to scientific research and made important contributions to anthropology.

Cole's rendition of Ruth Landes's work not only highlights the disposition of her research and writing in the anthropological canon, but also reveals a particular kind of "historical consciousness" that can emerge through the rereading of ethnographic insights. In her words, "An historical consciousness reveals that unsettling the concept of culture or, as I have termed it, writing against writing culture has long been a subtext in anthropology. It was part of the antiracist work of pre–World War II Boasians; it was central to the work of historical materialists (like Eleanor Leacock); and it is the project of contemporary feminists and ethnographers" (Cole 1995, 181). Through Cole's rereading of an early ethnography on race and gender, we are made aware of the complexity and heterogeneity of African-based cultures in relation to other cultures and anthropological insights. Cole's theoretical and methodological orientation is one of the most inspiring dimensions of her rereading of Landes's work. For Cole, rereading an early ethnographer like Landes unsettles taken-for-granted approaches to writing culture and contributes to the development of an "historical consciousness." This theoretical and methodological orientation is sensitive to the temporal and political location of Landes's writing and underscores how Landes's unconventional research avoided the cataloging of culture found within mainstream, professional anthropology at the time.

Like Cole's concern with the positionality of researchers in their ethnographic work and writing, Phillips (1996) considers some of the methodological problems associated with studying development and social change in the context of women's work and lives. She focuses on our role as researchers, the methods of engaging in research, and the political implications of our participation in the lives of women. She provides informative illustrations from her extensive work in rural Ecuador to contextualize her understanding of postcolonial methodologies. In an effort to be accountable as a researcher and sensitive to the needs of women and their interests, Phillips calls for researchers to be "reflexive about our own views, categories and contexts" and aware that the voices we draw upon are "our inventions" (1996, 27–28). A central issue that she deals with is the manner in which researchers might work through some of the assumptions contained within the methodology of placing women's voices at the center of development and on the pages of the researchers' written prose. Phillips argues that researchers must document the location and the positionality of the researcher and the way in which she participates in the lives of women and gives life to their voices in textual narration. As she states, researchers need to

explore and make explicit their *theory of listening*. Listening should not be taken for granted as a non-judgmental process; it is, like any social activity, a process steeped in ideologies that need to be explicitly examined if we are to avoid the old development traps. A theory of listening would tell us what researchers think is important, why they might think so, and how they have played a role in ensuring that the reader will agree with them when they make women's voices central to their projects. (1996, 21)

That researchers need to make explicit their "theory of listening" bears similarity to Stewart's emphasis on the processes involved in listening to others and in recollecting things ephemeral yet tactile, empirical, and imaginary (1996). The missing pieces and unknown meanings that Stewart confronted as she engaged in a research process of remembering and retelling taught her to "listen in order to retell." This type of listening, in turn, gave her the ability to recognize patterns in modes of telling, to follow along with stories and remember them, to tell stories in a local *way with words*, and to imagine the epistemological effects of a narrativized culture (1996, 8).

Researchers not only need to contextualize the voices of people that appear in their pages and to recognize the privileged position of researchers in terms of their ability to produce and displace knowledge, but also need, according to Phillips (1996), to give attention to the whole process of translation. This process involves the way in which words are translated from one language to another; the kinds of decisions that are made by the researcher when transforming oral conversations into text; and the manner in which women's voices are translated into women's interests. Translation is a very influential ethnographic practice, as Phillips (1996) suggests, and one that many researchers regularly use in ethnographic writing but whose implications or consequences they rarely explain.

Although we are generally sitting when we write, writing itself is not a stationary activity. In ethnographic writing, translation reflects acts of movement, of "telling and retelling" stories (Stewart 1996), of rendering and rewording, of building and revising, and of forming and transforming. In this field, the writer establishes relations between things and proceeds from one person's story to another, from one place to another, and from one condition to another. It is through translation that local issues can become tied to larger ones (Rose and Miller 1992, 177). While translation may build from imperfect equivalences, dwell in approximations that privilege certain "originals" framed for particular audiences (Clifford 1997, 11), or be a part of "ethnographic authority" (Su 1999, 34), it is a process that can displace other knowledge at the same time that the writer can be displaced by this knowledge. This practice hints at other circuits of travel that researchers become entwined in.

Aihwa Ong alerts us to the specific circuits of travel of the researcher and those diasporic Chinese women who struggle for emancipation. In "Women Out of China: Traveling Tales and Traveling Theories in Postcolonial Feminism," Ong (1995) is concerned with the reproduction of colonial domination in academic writing. One of her focal points is the political implications of researching and writing about people's lives who are less privileged. In this context, she confronts the issue of whether we can truly represent less privileged peoples. She questions whether researchers, implicated in a relation of power, can learn to listen well and to convey informants' stories without political betrayal. She presents two detailed Chinese immigrant women's tales of emigration that revolve around changing stereotypical Western perceptions of Chinese immigrant women. These women describe how they have created a home for themselves in diaspora through their reflections on overseas Chinese communities and Chinese family strategies. These descriptions bear similarity to the way that African-descended peoples have imagined the meaning of homeland as they dwell in diaspora (see Gilroy 1993) and to the way that Behar in *The Vulnerable Observer* talks about Cuban diaspora as a site for the re-creation of both identity and memory (1996, 142–147).

For Ong, a relationship exists between the experiences of diaspora and the development of an emerging agency. Immigrant women's autobiographic accounts express an emerging agency. Ong believes that this emerging agency can challenge feminist theories of postcolonial women by providing researchers with knowledge about postcolonialism from different geopolitical sites. From this perspective, she asserts that the power dimension associated with the making of ethnography does not derive from "our position and embodiment as postcolonial analysts as from recognition of an interreferencing sensibility that we share with less privileged postcolonial women" (Ong 1995, 367). She adds that this common ground of a decentered cultural/political relationship to the West can foster a more equitable kind of listening and retelling. This is because researchers can become, for Ong, a channel for the voices of postcolonial women that would allow women greater opportunity to form a counterpoint to hegemonic narratives.

At one level, I would agree that it is important to document less privileged postcolonial women's lives and experiences through the making of ethnography. At another level, however, it is too presumptuous to make the claim that ethnographers can challenge hegemonic narratives through postcolonial women's voices. Postcolonial women's language or their experiences may not easily lend themselves to actions on the part of an ethnographer. Furthermore, it is not necessarily the case that postcolonial women would in fact want ethnographers to challenge hegemonic narratives on *their* behalf. If anything, I believe that studying and engaging with postcolonial women's lives can potentially provide some interesting lessons for feminist scholarship. It may also provide critical insights for thinking about issues of change and agency in feminist scholarship more broadly.

What is most compelling about the work of Cole (1995, 1999), Phillips (1996), Stewart (1996), and Ong (1995) is that these ethnographers are grappling with methodological issues surrounding ethnographic practices. In illustrating the wide-ranging political implications of engaging in ethnographic research, they take seriously the positionality of researchers to their participants and to their own written work.

This chapter has attempted to illustrate the interrelations of habitation and movement in contemporary ethnography. By refusing to settle on culture as "something" rooted in space and time, I have focused on the mobile dimensions of culture in ethnographic practices. These dimensions embody the transformation of worlds and words, the interacting forms of research and writing, and the poetics and politics of ethnographic lives. Through a mobile sensitivity that awakes to a life of stories, events, and places in transit, I have woven in my stories of how migratory groupings signal particular spaces and times, bring together memory and longing, and intermingle the local with the global. I have shown how people's lives dwell in transportable relations and not in fixed structures. For me, this focus on mobility has the potential to alert us to a wide range of social practices, stories, and events that distinguish lives in transition. It also has the potential to alert researchers to a form of research and writing that does not focus on one bounded situation but allows for fluid dimensions of culture to come more sharply into view. This analytic focus may well help in overcoming the limitations associated with settling people and their practices. Like this chapter, the following chapter concentrates on another form of transit and transition. It highlights diasporas in the twentieth century and their various forms of marginalization and disengagement in different "homelands." It focuses on post–World War II migrant and immigrant workforces in Germany and provides an extended focus on guest workers and their lives away from home.

NOTES

1. See Barrett (1999) for an excellent discussion of disciplinary considerations, such as the shifting of "appropriate" subject matter and the export of methods and techniques.

2. The Birmingham School, comprised of a group of sociologists and other academics and activists connected to the Centre for Contemporary Cultural Studies, is known for their research on communities of class and ethnicity and specifically for their focus on the cultural practices of resistance.

3. For an insightful discussion of morality and the practices of veiling in Yemen, see Meneley (2000).

4. While I have indicated that displacement is full of indeterminancy and contradictions, Ferguson (1999, 153) warns that there is a temptation to understand the idea of displacement as a specific social condition that follows from some definitive break with a social life rooted in ancestral places.

CHAPTER 4

BORDER PASSAGES

In this chapter, I concentrate on a form of movement, of transit and transition, that extends my earlier discussions on the topic to new fields of inquiry. I draw attention to diasporas in the twentieth century, to those dispersed networks of people who experience displacement and adjustment in different "homelands." By way of illustration, and in the context of resettlement, I focus on post–World War II diasporic guest workers in Western Europe and offer a detailed analysis of the German guest worker system. I examine issues relating to the recruitment of guest workers to the "host" country, the bilateral agreements between Germany and the "guest" countries, and the regulation of guest workers through policies and programs, and develop these issues through an extended analysis of Turkish guest workers in Germany. Since the early 1960s, Turkish migrants constitute the largest group of guest workers in Germany. Their migration occurred at a time when the Turkish state and economy were facing economic and political crises.

Given the perceived unruliness linked to such diasporic groups, and the growing importance of national belonging, I illustrate how the German state directs their movements to, within, and out of Germany. Their movements are controlled through residential and work permits, immigration policies, and naturalization laws based upon descent. These control mechanisms, which reflect the state's engagement in activities of individualization, serve to produce and reproduce the cultural and economic marginality of these diasporic groups. The cultural distinctiveness of these groups is echoed in their personal and poetic descriptions of their location in *gurbet*, that is, in their perceived state of exile, and in their longing for belonging. Based upon a wide array of diasporic articulations, I argue that diaspora neither develops from rooted communities nor are its characteristics derived from the experience of individuals or groups in isolation. Instead, diaspora is constituted through the combined cultural and political processes of migration and "othering."

DISPLACEMENT AND RELOCATION

> The emergence of 20th-century diasporas delinks identity and culture from one's immediate locale or neighbourhood and disrupts the anchoring of culture in the landscape, material culture and face-to-face encounters.
> —R. Shields, "Culture and the Economy of Cities" (1999, 306)

> Diasporas entail the notion that the "old country" where one is no longer living, exerts some claim upon one's loyalties, emotions and identity. Such an old country can be defined in terms of language, religion, customs or folklore. All diasporic communities are thus in part cultural.
> —J. Urry, *Sociology Beyond Societies* (2000a, 154–155)

Diasporas are dispersed networks of peoples who share common historical experiences of dispossession, displacement, and adjustment (Clifford 1997, 253). While they have value in terms of their economic contributions, and in the demand for migrant or immigrant workforces that call for the import and export of diasporic groups, their economic value bespeaks a life instilled with regulatory discourses and strategies of direction that are both more imperatively coordinated and more pervasive than ever before.

While nations take comfort in their images of justice and democracy, these same images can obscure the poverty, violence, or gender conflicts faced by diasporic "communities" because of the dominant presumption that communities are culturally and politically homogeneous (see Bauman 2001b). In addition to their economic value, diasporas also have another utility to the nation. This value is ideological. Indeed, many nation-states have an ideological dependence on diaspora, and this more insidious utility is very much alive. We often learn of it in the deliberations on morality and ethics, in matters of violence, in fears of the "other," and in themes of national distinctiveness, whether of blood or soil (see Chavez 2001; Malkki 1999). In these deliberations, there is rarely a concern for diasporic peoples themselves and the processes of "othering" experienced by them. For example, diasporic groups are often perceived as criminogenic or are placed at the origins of immorality. Liisa Malkki illustrates how refugees who lost their national homeland after World War II were identified by policymakers and scholars of the time as a politico-moral problem. She cites a prominent 1939 survey of refugees that states: "Politically uprooted, he [the refugee] may sink into the underworld of terrorism and political crime; and in any case he is suspected of political irresponsibility that endangers national security" (1999, 62). Other similar accounts depict refugees' loss of connection to their national homelands as a loss of moral bearing. In the postwar literature, refugees posed a problem of individual or personal responsibility rather than a problem of "the political conditions and processes that produce massive territorial displacements of people" (Malkki 1999, 63).

Diasporic groups have not only been subject to moral criticism, but they have also been formally alienated from "naturalization" based upon descent. The German law on national citizenship is one prime example of where this alienation occurs. The law grants nationality according to the "law of the blood" (in Latin, *jus sanguinis*), to those who have German parents rather than to those who are born in Germany. By virtue of this principle, German nationality is acquired only by the descent of a male German national and, since 1974, by the descent of a female German (Rittstieg 1994, 114). The "law of the blood" dates back to a time when the German *Reich* emerged as the first German national state in 1871. Membership rooted in descent was one way to deal with the fact that enhanced mobility made it "more and more difficult to determine who belonged and who did not, and helped states 'hold onto' population temporarily—or even permanently—living elsewhere than within the state's territorial boundaries" (Torpey 2000, 72). Far from being democratic, the constitutional "law of the blood" relied more on subjects than on citizens. Prior to this historical juncture, nationality was defined through ethnicity as established by language and culture. The "law of the blood" meant that only by being born into the German community could a person acquire the status of a German national. In this regard, "blood" became a marker of ethnicity. As Castles and Miller argue, "when Hitler annexed Austria in 1938, he could claim that its people were coming 'home to the *Reich*,' though they had never actually belonged to it. The same principle was used to take citizenship away from Jews and gypsies whose ancestors had lived on German soil for centuries" (1998, 202). This was the ideological background of the nationality statute (*jus sanguinis*) passed in 1913, the principles of which govern German nationality to this day. Since German citizenship is legally reckoned through blood rather than place, "being born 'German' links you not only to your father, mother, grandparents but in an extended sense to all other Germans before you" (Peck 1995, 112). Perhaps more significant, granting German citizenship based on blood has unsettled generations of immigrants and refugees who have lived and who have given birth to children in the country for the past several decades. It is no wonder that German nationalism is vilified so strongly in the genre of *Gastarbeiterliteratur* (migrant and refugee literature). Over the years, this literature has, among other things, challenged the nation-state as the central source of citizenship authority (See Isin 2000 for more on the practices of citizenship).

In the twentieth century, most every community has dimensions of un-settlement associated with it. These dimensions accentuate how migrant groups feel when they confront the loss of a past "home," become tangled between indeterminate pasts and futures, and have social ties to more than one place. This is particularly the case as ethnic expulsion, migration, changing places, and leaving home are experiences for more and more people in modernity (see chapter 5).[1] For example, after the collapse of the Nazi regime at the end of World War II, millions of displaced persons drifted across Europe, including forced laborers from the East in Germany, inmates of concentration camps, and deported Germans in communist countries. Some 1,496,000 ethnic Poles and Polish Jews were compelled to leave their traditional settlements in former Eastern Poland, which is now part of Lithuania, Belorussia, and the Ukraine. Approximately twelve mil-lion ethnic Germans either fled or were displaced from the eastern parts of the former *Reich* and the territories previously occupied by the German *Wehrmacht* (Poland, the Baltics, Bohemia, Moravia, Slovenia, Serbia, and the Ukraine) (Fassmann and Münz 1994, 521–523). After World War II, the Czechoslovakian state developed a policy of forceful sedentarization of "gypsy" populations and their integration with the Czechs. This policy dispersed and resettled the population in housing estates that were left va-cant after the expulsion of the German minority (Holy 1998, 133).

If these post–World War II displacements do not give us a sense of di-aspora, then we might consider the more recent decades of global popu-lation movements that have come to impact a wide array of minority groups. We continue to read about the displacement, eviction, flight, and refugee or noncitizen status that characterize the lives of millions of Kurdish people around the world. Also, with the end of the Cold War and German reunification, massive shifts in populations that have taken place since 1989 have signaled a broad new wave of labor mobility (see Carnoy 2000, 63) and have made immigration and ethnic diversity central political issues. Likewise, the breakup of the Soviet Union since 1991 has been accompa-nied by a vast population movement wherein millions of people of various ethnic backgrounds have been pressured to relocate and become "foreigners overnight" (Van Hear 1998, 24–25). With the ongoing displacement of particular groups, I pose the following question: How do we conceive of dispersed migrant or minority peoples who may be separated from home-lands by political barriers, who may increasingly find themselves recollect-ing and longing for past ways of life and lifestyles, or who may return, temporarily or permanently, to their homelands?

While the displacement of peoples is not anything new in modernity, there are ways of understanding the practices of long-term dwelling away from home that do not revolve around moral judgments or criminogenic behavior. For example, Safran (1991) sees diaspora as involving a history of dispersal, memories or myths of the homeland, alienation in the host country, desire for eventual return, ongoing support of the homeland, and a collective identity defined by a continuing relationship with the homeland. From Safran's perspective, collective identity is not rendered in terms of origins, tradition, or territory, but in terms of an historically lived experience of social mobility. In *Routes: Travel and Translation in the Late Twentieth Century*, Clifford (1997) takes issue with Safran's "centered" diasporic model, a model oriented by continuous cultural connections to a source and by a teleology of "return" to an original homeland. He makes the argument that this model cannot accommodate the experiences of African American or Caribbean cultures. Instead, he suggests that there is a range of diasporas, of dispersed networks of people who share common historical experiences of dispossession and displacement. Consequently, he argues that decentered lateral connections for diasporic groups may be as important as those formed around a teleology of return. For Clifford, the term "diaspora" is "a signifier not simply of transnationality and movement but of political struggles to define the local, as distinctive community, in historical contexts of displacement" (1997, 252). His theory of diaspora explains how movement complicates the concept of nativeness or rootedness as more and more people become chronically mobile and are routinely displaced from territorial or national places. This displacement process forces us to think again about the ways in which "homes" and "homelands" are constructed by dispersed networks of people.

Margins and borders are increasingly at the focal point of inquiries into the movements of displaced peoples. Dispersed networks of people bring to the fore both the dissimilarities and convergences between home settings and new locations. Complementing Clifford's emphasis on the relationship between diaspora and transnationalism, Gupta and Ferguson (1999b) suggest that with the mass movements of populations and of capital flows, the familiar lines between "here" and "there," center and periphery, colony and metropole become blurred. The development of eclipsed boundaries and borders necessarily means that there are other, complex relations that encompass displaced peoples and their experiences of displacement. On this point, we may recall the millions of inhabitants who not only lost their homes in the former republic of Yugoslavia but had to flee from the war in 1991 that tore Yugoslavia apart (see Jansen 1998). Situations like this clarify why "people remaining in familiar and ancestral places find the nature of their relation to place ineluctably changed and the illusion of a natural and essential connection between place and the culture broken" (Gupta and Ferguson 1999b, 38). As Gupta and Ferguson suggest, the attendance of such changing times and places calls for a stronger focus on the processes by which place and homeland are constructed by mobile populations. They give examples of how "remembered places" serve as symbolic anchors of community for dispersed people, such as immigrants and refugees, and of how the relation to homeland can be constructed differently in different settings. This leads the authors to focus on the processes of the "production of difference" in the interconnected and interdependent spaces of culture, society, and economy. In this discussion they indicate that space and place are never given but always produced, imagined, resisted, or enforced.

Following Gupta and Ferguson's emphasis on the complexities of displaced peoples (1999b), I approach diaspora as a process of unsettlement and movement experienced by people who are forced to migrate from their homeland, or who are drawn into new places to live and work, and who require new habits and responsibilities. My purpose here is to draw attention to how diaspora underscores the combined relations of migration and otherness that characterize particular displaced and uprooted peoples, such as the *gastarbeiter*s or *ausländer*s in Germany. These relations become frequently entangled in state programs and policies of immigration or assimilation that direct the spatial and temporal movements of diasporic groups. Diasporic relations alert us to the complex ways in which migrant populations experience exile and the longing that resides with and within belonging. They also alert us to the manner in which populations are individualized in modern society by social processes, strategies, and techniques (see Bauman 2000, 30–38).

UNSETTLING HABITS: THE GASTARBEITER

> The displaced do not experience temporary absences only to be confirmed in the well-ordered structure of normal life. Theirs is a more or less permanent experience of not being *in situ* as they negotiate a diversity of experiences in a deterritorialized world.
>
> —K. Fog Olwig, "Cultural Sites" (1997, 34)

The post–World War II guest workers in Europe exemplify diaspora beset by the dimensions and tensions of unsettlement. In their economic function, guest workers were accepted into other countries as a source of cheap labor. Those migrant workforces, from Mediterranean countries in particular, were a consequence of the economic expansionism (including the shift to new methods of mass production) that swept through the industrialized countries in Western Europe. The main countries to receive these migrant workers were Germany, Belgium, Great Britain, France, Switzerland, and the Netherlands.

The Federal Republic of Germany (FRG) is a prime example of the guest worker system in terms of its strategies of ethnic segregation and surveillance. This guest worker system recruited manual workers to work in factories and low-skilled jobs in various sectors of the national economy. The official import of migrant workers to Germany began with a formal bilateral agreement signed by Germany and Italy in 1955. Many other, similar bilateral agreements followed thereafter: 1960, Spain and Greece; 1961, Turkey; 1963, Morocco; 1964, Portugal; 1965, Tunisia; and 1969, Yugoslavia (Peck 1995, 114).[2] These bilateral agreements regulated the movement and recruitment of guest workers between the host and sending countries. The German Federal Labor Office (*Bundesanstalt für Arbeit*, or BfA) set up recruitment offices in Mediterranean countries. German employers requiring immigrant labor engaged in a fee-for-service contract with the BfA. For this fee, the BfA was responsible for selecting workers, testing occupational abilities, providing medical checkups, and screening police records. When workers were brought to Germany, often in groups, employers were responsible for the provision of initial accommodation in hostels or camps located near work sites. German guest worker policies envisioned these migrant workers as temporary labor units that could be recruited, utilized, and dismissed as the economy demanded. For migrants to enter and remain in Germany they needed both a residence and a labor permit. Labor permits were supplied only for those jobs that held no interest for German and European Economic Community (EEC) workers, were granted only for restricted periods, and were valid only for specific jobs in certain regions. Though initially the entry of dependents was discouraged, competition with other labor-importing countries for labor led to the relaxation of restrictions on the entry of dependents in the 1960s (Castles and Miller 1998, 71).[3]

Many nations now confront regular influxes of immigrants, migrants, and refugees. Sometimes these groups are welcomed. However, in many cases they have been relegated to the margins of mainstream society through strategies of national and environmental racism, institutional racism, ethnic violence, or ethnic cleansing (see, e.g., Torpey 2000; Diken 1998; Appadurai 1996, 173; Castles and Miller 1998). For the most part, guest workers in Germany have been less than welcomed and far more affected by state mechanisms for regulating and authorizing their movements. In the German case, the state has monopolized the authority to direct the movements of diasporic groups, such as guest workers. Since it is believed that these groups do not have any direction of their own, the German state—through a whole series of bureaucratic strategies and tactics—has regulated their movements to, within, and out of the country. This has been accomplished through the deployment of residential and work permits; policies pertaining to impermissible offenses on the part of "foreigners" (e.g., threatening the safety of the country; endangering public health or morals); and enforcement of various family, immigration, and asylum laws. For example, the Federal Labor Office organized the recruitment of guest workers and granted their work permits. The *Ausländerpol-*

izei (foreigners police) issued residence permits, kept foreign workers under surveillance, and deported those who transgressed the regulations, such as those who switched to better-paying jobs without obtaining approval (Castles and Miller 1998, 203). These are some of the ways that state bureaucracies have regulated the movement of diaspora.

A number of other policies and programs have controlled guest workers' place and status in Germany. For example, the Aliens Act of 1965 (*Ausländergesetz*), enacted in conjunction with the Promotion of Labor Act of 1969 (*Arbeitsförderungsgesetz*), offered ground rules but no definition of guest workers' formal legal status in Germany. Subsequent legislation to regulate guest workers included a national hiring freeze and a labor importation ban in 1973; a revised Aliens Act in 1975; alterations in the cutoff dates for admitting family and dependents in 1979; and a resolution concerning the visa status of children over sixteen in 1981 (Mushaben 1985, 127–128). In 1983 a policy of selective displacement prevailed. Largely unsuccessful, this policy aimed to reduce the number of foreign workers in Germany by granting them financial incentives to return to their homelands (Castles and Miller 1998).

The idea of belonging that is at the core of the concept of citizenship is threatened when people, such as migrant workers, cross borders. The rules of citizenship, of who deserves the protection and rights guaranteed by the state, remain a thorny problem for many so-called foreigners and guest workers in Germany. A ten-year period of legal residence, language proficiency, integration into German society, and other conditions (e.g., basic knowledge of the political order; sufficient income to support a family; etc.) are the common requirements for the acquisition of discretionary naturalization today (see Çinar 1994, 51). Current nationality requirements are not what they were in earlier years. By the end of the 1970s, "the integration of foreigners" was a declared government policy, one that emerged alongside the decision to withhold German nationality for ethnic Germans. This integration policy meant that guest workers and their children had to integrate as "foreigners." In this context, as Rittstieg claims, "integration implies that the immigrant accepts the discrimination connected with the status of a foreigner permanently for him and his offspring" (1994, 112). By the mid-1980s, over three million "foreigners" fulfilled the ten-year residence qualification but far less than 1 percent per year actually obtained citizenship.[4] In the 1990s, the rules of naturalization were made easier[5] but the rate of naturalization remains low in relation to Germany's large "foreign" population. For example, children born in Germany to foreign parents do not have an automatic right to citizenship. Second-generation immigrants can be deported under certain circumstances (such as conviction for criminal offenses or long-term unemployment). Even the third generation (children born to parents who were themselves born in Germany of immigrant parents) are not automatically German, although new policies

introduced in 1993 do give the third generation a strong claim to naturalization (Castles and Miller 1998, 202). Many immigrant workers and their
families are not citizens and therefore are not entitled to vote. This fact has
worked to the benefit of right-wing conservative parties, and is particularly
significant given that parties on the left are aided, in part, by the support
of working-class groups of which migrant workers form a part. In this
regard, the concept of citizenship is the object of ongoing political struggles
and a critical component of a broader "historical matrix of governance"
(Brodie 2000b, 111). Furthermore, the difficulty in obtaining citizenship
for foreign migrant workers and their families is only one of several other
administrative issues that these groups face.

Similar to the way that the terms "black," "Indian," or "Asian" were
applied to diasporic groups in Britain (see Brah 1991), foreign migrant
workers in Germany are, and have been, administratively defined by terms
of "othering." Over time, these terms have ranged from *fremdarbeiter*
(alien workers), to *gastarbeiter* (guest workers), to *ausländsroboter* (foreign
robots) and *ausländische arbeitnehmer* (foreign employees) (Bendix 1985,
29–30). Not only do these terms create new social divisions, but they also
reflect the manner in which migrant groups are considered to lack a place
and roots in a "host" nation and its history. Jeffery Peck (1995) argues
that the German authorities distinguish foreigner groups in order to grant
specific groups, such as those who are not *ausländer* (lit., "from outside
the country"), certain privileges and rights and, I would add, much more
economic and political mobility than migrant populations.

MIGRANTS IN TRANSITION: THE TURKISH "AUSLÄNDER"

> Another word in my mother tongue once came to me in a dream. A
> train travels along, stops, outside they're making arrests, dogs bark,
> three ticket collectors come, I consider whether I should say, "I am
> Italian." I want to hide my passport, which lists my profession as IŞCI
> [meaning "worker" in Turkish]. I think if I can say that I am a student
> or an artist, I'll get through the inspection. There's a photocopier there
> as big as a room, it prints a very large self-portrait of me as an IŞCI.
> —E. Sevgi Özdamar, *Mother Tongue* (1994, 13)

> We sweep the streets of foreign cities, hands filthy, hearts filthy.
> —F. Hüsnü Dağlarca, "Our Street-Sweepers in Germany"
> (cited in Halman 1985, 86)

The largest group of guest workers in Germany is from Turkey. Like
other similar groups, this group is labeled by the German term *ausländer*.
In 1961 an official agreement between Germany and Turkey initiated the

movement of Turkish workers (predominately males) to Germany.[6] Upon their relocation from villages and towns of Turkey to cities in West Germany (and to other cities in Belgium, Holland, and Austria), Turkish migrant workers engaged in work in German manufacturing and construction industries as well as in catering and domestic services.

The initial migration of Turkish workers to Germany occurred during a time when Turkish society was encountering both economic and political crises, including soaring inflation, high unemployment rates, and large external debts. As a way to overcome such crises, the Turkish state initiated many changes, including the introduction of rapid industrialization policies based on the model of import substitution; the regulation of working-class revolts and trade-union movements; and the transformation of dispossessed peasants into a large migrant population (see Berberoğlu 1982, 89–97; Ahmad 1993, 133). At this historical, economic, and political juncture, just over three-quarters of Turkey's population participated in agricultural production. In 1963, for example, 41 percent of the national income and over 80 percent of exports were derived from agricultural products, such as cotton, tobacco, dried fruit, and nuts (Kocturk 1992, 86; Paine 1974, 30). Although agricultural production was the mainstay of the Turkish economy, a large-scale exodus of people from rural to urban areas was already well under way in the 1950s. The exodus of rural peoples was prompted by their forced displacement from small-scale farming as a result of the mechanization and capitalization of farming, their continued poverty, and their insufficient access to arable land. The proliferation of urban industries and the development of an informal economy in city centers enabled some workers to engage in both farming and seasonal migrant occupations or to leave farming altogether for urban wage labor (see Ilcan 1994). It is against this historical background that workers migrated from Turkey to Germany.[7]

Within a decade following the initial migration of a relatively small number of Turkish workers to Germany, a huge increase in the export of migrant workers occurred. In 1966 the number of Turkish migrant workers employed in Germany totaled just over 160,000 (Penninx 1982, 786). By the late 1960s to the early 1970s, 525,000 Turkish laborers were exported to European economies, particularly to the German economy. For Turkey, the exiting of workers resulted in decreases in unemployment rates and increases in monetary remittances from Turkish workers to their families back home.[8] The latter, in particular, enabled the country to import capital goods and raw materials for its industries and "maintain an equilibrium in the balance of payments" (Ahmad 1993, 133). It was at this time that large numbers of Turkish women and children also migrated to Germany (and to other European countries) to join their husbands or family members. This movement facilitated an increase in the proportion of female workers in Germany. However, these female workers entered industrial jobs with no experience of city life, disciplined working hours, or industrial work environments.[9] As they held paid employment, they also continued their domestic work responsibilities at home. This paid and unpaid work forced female migrants to negotiate productive and reproductive work relations in a deterritorialized environment that was markedly different from their life in village communities, where there they could rely on economic and social support from kin and neighborhood networks. While the Turkish female migrant population in Germany increased, the economic and political crises in Turkey continued. Between 1973 and 1979, two military takeovers took place and thirteen coalition governments were formed (Berberoğlu 1982, 108–109). As a consequence, between 1972 and 1983, many Turkish "involuntary migrants"[10] or refugees sought asylum in Germany and in other European countries (Kocturk 1992, 86–92).[11]

Like other diasporic groups, Turkish diasporas and their family members have found it difficult to become citizens of the German state. This difficulty has been articulated in numerous public political debates and in large antiracist demonstrations throughout Germany following the murder of several Turks in arson attacks in Mölln in 1991 and Solingen in 1993. The demand for dual citizenship was one of the main issues raised in these debates and demonstrations. Dual citizenship is an important issue for many Turkish migrant workers and their families, as they cannot easily give up their Turkish citizenship and all the rights and privileges that this grants them.

According to Germany's New Aliens Act of 1991, long-term residents are now entitled to acquire German citizenship if certain conditions are met. Since 1993 this entitlement has been strengthened. Immigrants who have been residing in the Federal Republic for at least fifteen years are allowed to apply for German citizenship on the conditions that they have sufficient private income, give up their previous citizenship, and have not been convicted of a crime (Çinar 1994, 54–55; Rittstieg 1994, 114–115). Though the Aliens Act makes the renouncement of one's former nationality a condition of naturalization, there are exceptions to this rule. Immigrants may receive German nationality and keep their former nationality if all the other above-mentioned conditions are fulfilled and if "the laws or practice of the state of their nationality make it impossible to renounce this nationality, or . . . the conditions to renounce nationality are disproportionate or arbitrary, or . . . delays are unreasonable, or . . . the precondition for the renouncement of nationality is the completion of military service and the young man who wants to naturalize has grown up in Germany" (Rittstieg 1994, 115). Nevertheless, as few as 1 percent of Turks established in Germany have received, or have been allowed to take, citizenship (see Atalık and Beeley 1993, 169). On this front, Ignatieff alerts us to the tensions between nation and belonging:

the legal instruments that define German identity remain defined by the ethnic national past. The criterion of citizenship remains one of ethnic descent on the basis of *jus sanguinis* [the "law of the blood"]. The resulting contradiction between reality and ethnic fantasy produces manifest unreason. To most outsiders, and to many Germans, it seems absurd that a Turk born and brought up in Germany should be unable to become a citizen, while a German from Siberia, with no history of residence in the country and little language competence, should be entitled to citizenship and to extensive settlement assistance. (1993, 101)

Ignatieff reminds us of how peoples' right to a state can be mediated by their membership in a specific ethnic group.

Like other diasporic groups, a large portion of the two million Turkish migrants and immigrants in Germany have been resettled to the political and economic margins of German society. Dating back to the early 1960s, Turkish migrant workers obtained entry-level industrial jobs that were perceived as temporary, as the term *gastarbeiter* implies. This temporary residence framework still shapes their social and economic status today. Different from their relatively high rate of employment in the 1960s and 1970s, Turkish migrants have been economically marginalized through insecure work, low pay, and frequent unemployment or underemployment since the early 1980s. For example, the unemployment rate for Turkish residents in 1995 was just over 24 percent, compared with only 9.3 percent for the workforce as a whole (Castles and Miller 1998, 195). Not only are they economically marginalized, but they are also often politically marginalized as a consequence of their on-going efforts to influence government decisions about their political and economic status in a context of escalating streams of racism and right-wing xenophobia, although they have resisted these streams of racism through mass appeals, public demonstrations, and the formation of Islamic and Turkish associations in Germany. Their economic and political marginalization is further exacerbated by their location in low-standard urban and suburban areas of Germany.

Depending on socio-economic factors, such as places of work, transport facilities, or housing prices (see Yuval-Davis 2000, 178), ethnic Turks are concentrated in neighborhoods that limit their access to social amenities (such as schools, healthcare facilities, and recreational facilities). These neighborhoods are diverse but remain separate from other German neighborhoods. The Turkish community of Kreuzberg in Berlin is a well-known case of residential and ethnic segregation. It contains an "ethnic" infrastructure of corner stores, coffee shops, retail businesses, and service agencies that cater to some of the needs of the Turkish population. The spatial dislocation of ethnic Turks in Kreuzberg reflects the tension of being within and between sets of social relations. It also alerts us to ways in which Turkish migrants and immigrants dwell in and sustain communities, develop networks, activities, patterns of living, and ideologies that span their home and the host society. Since the arrival of Turkish women and children in the 1970s, Germany witnessed the opening of Koran schools, mosques, and Turkish Islamic organizations, although, unlike Christian churches and organizations in Germany, no state subsidies are provided to Turkish religious or cultural organizations and therefore their political influence is limited (Doomernik 1995). Even though Turkish businesses,[12] establishments, and neighborhoods have sprung up in many German towns and city centers, these places are not devoid of the longing in belonging that many Turkish diasporas experience.

AT THE CROSSROADS

The Turkish diasporas that I have come to know while living in Germany and in the northwestern Turkish community of Saklı feel like they are in a "hostland" and not in a "homeland." Following Carol Delaney (1990), this feeling may well reflect their penetrating state of *gurbet*, a Turkish term that translates as "foreign land." It appears in the lyrics of numerous folk songs dedicated to the distress and difficulties of being away from "home." Voluminous writings on *gurbet* have developed into an "exile literature" (*gurbet edebiyati*), a "migrant literature" (*göç edebiyati*), or the literature of the "*gastarbeiter.*"[13] In its common uses, *gurbet* means exile from home and calls forth a sentiment of displacement. For Delaney, immigrant Turks are

strangers in a strange land, exiled not only among strangers but among people who do not share their language, religion, values, or customs. If home is where the heart is, then the village is the home for which they pine, a vital "center out there" pulling them in its direction and orienting their lives in space and time. Its location in space is known, and some immigrants boast that they know the way there by heart. It also organizes the temporal order, for the village exists as a frame of reference both "before" and "after" the sojourn in an alien land. (1990, 523)

Similar sentiments of *gurbet* are also experienced by those whom I visited during one of my research excursions to the community of Saklı, located in the province of Zonguldak. One guest worker, Ahmet, and his family talked with me at length while on their annual return trip from Germany. At the time of their return, I was living in Saklı and conducting research on the social history and transformation of the peasant economy and its cultural dimensions. Although international migration was not central to the goals of my research at that time, Ahmet alerted me the benefits and the problems of being an international migrant worker. In the company of his older brother, a retired international migrant coal miner who had also worked in Germany, Ahmet recollected some of the difficulties of living away from home:

There is no doubt that we [Turkish workers in Germany] are paid well for our work. You know how little the coal mines pay their workers in Zonguldak. I'm sure many people have already told you this. Look at the houses around here [referring to the two-story, concrete buildings that were "built from deutsche Marks"]. Who could afford to build them except for people like us who work in Germany. It would be impossible for us to earn this kind of money in the coal mines here. Thanks to God, I am pleased that we are able to share our benefits with our relatives here.

Before visiting Ahmet and his family, I had the opportunity to speak with many retired migrant workers living in Saklı and to hear their stories. I remembered their tales of living away from their homeland, especially their search for a place to call home from the visible walls of ethnic ghettos, from a sea of turbulence and inhospitality, and from a national milieu of enforced belonging. With these place-images of migrancy in mind, I asked Ahmet what it was like being away from his *memleket* (country). He responded by saying:

We pay a price for being away from home. We miss our *memleket, mahalle* [neighborhood], *akraba* [relatives], our way of life here. . . . As you know, we are unable to attend many family events in our village because of being away. We can only leave Germany and come home once a year. But, we will come back here soon, permanently, *inşallah* [if god wills]. . . . It is a difficult life for us in Germany. We work hard. Our wives also work. You can call what they do as work too. They work inside the home; they look after our children and raise them to be proud of our country, proud of being Turkish. . . . Generally, I can say that our life there is about work, a lot of hard work. Who do we really have there besides my younger brother and his family? I have many Turkish friends there. But after all the years I have lived in Germany, I only have one or two German friends. The German people really don't understand us; they don't know our culture; they don't know our land; they don't speak our language; they don't know anything about "our roots" [*bizim kökler*, meaning "our ancestors"]. How are we supposed to understand each other? This is why there will always be conflict, conflict between them and us.

The community of Saklı where Ahmet was born in is an expansive mountainous area. Its population is just under six hundred and its laborers engage in subsistence farming and in local and international migrant wage work. Saklı's eighty-some households are assembled in four distinct descent-based neighborhoods that carry the traces of the memories of different social groups who have lived in or passed through them historically. With the exception of the few landlord families who own the majority of land in the area and rent portions of it to local and nearby residents, most village neighborhoods are poor and lack sufficient land access.

Diverse forms of mobility characterize these neighborhoods. A significant number of males leave their descent-based neighborhoods to engage in migrant labor in the nearby coal-mining operations in Zonguldak. They return home to their families on the weekends. Since the early 1970s, long-term and permanent out-migration has resulted in the relocation of villagers (from about twenty-five Saklı households) to Germany. In Germany, male villagers engage in coal mining and factory work and often maintain residence in Saklı. While residing in Germany, they send remittances to their relatives, as Ahmet does. Other workers have returned permanently to their neighborhoods after working in Germany for many years. They have added large extensions to their village homes. In fact, whenever a house has more than one story, it is taken as a sign that the owners worked in Germany. The largest and oldest descent neighborhood in Saklı contains numerous two-story homes. This neighborhood, once renowned for its warmth and friendliness prior to the out-migration of some of its members, has the highest proportion of males working in Germany and in Zonguldak's coal-mining industry. Now it is colored with the reputation of being inhospitable (*soğuk*, unfriendly). Defined by its closely watched borders, the neighborhood is viewed by others as a place that has been disorganized (*karışlık*) by the lifestyles and outlooks of migrant workers. The influence of "outside" German forces is considered by most villagers to account for major changes in *komşuluk* (neighborliness). These outside forces are also considered to contribute to the changes in the meaning of local time, that is, where social movements are no longer punctuated by the social activities of birth and death, planting and harvesting, visiting and receiving neighbors, the tasks entailed in going to the market, the duty of engaging in daily prayers, and so on. In fact, those who left this neighborhood for paid labor in Germany are now referred to as *Almanyalı* (those from Germany). This term was coined by the rural peoples who have stayed behind and maintained, from their perspective, their ancestral ties to the land and the people. It is a term that is commonly used throughout Turkey to refer to those Turks who return "home" from Germany (see Atalık and Beeley 1993, 168–169).

Descent reckoning in many communities in Turkey, including that of Saklı, plays an important role in assembling and disassembling groups around a myth of origin or beginning. It bears similarity to the way that some nation-states, such as Germany, use ancestry or blood ties to grant people the status of German citizenship and, therefore, certain rights and privileges. In various regions of Turkey the identification of one's origins involves the tracing of one's *kök* ("roots" or ancestry). *Kök* is the common term used to discuss descent. People trace their lineage to and from their patrilineal ancestors, their *ata* (father-ancestor) or *dede* (grandfather), and, in this way, *kök* is reckoned exclusively through a chain of father–child linkages. For example, the *kök* of one's mother is traced through her father and her father's father. In Saklı, community residents maintain that any two people who share a common ancestor possess a continuity in the past, present, and future, and are kin.

Descending from a common *kök* contributes to the formation of neighborhoods whose members may share lifestyles and often own property or resources in common. However, not all people who live in descent-based neighborhoods hold the same rights or privileges. Women who move to such neighborhoods upon marriage and take up postmarital virilocal residence neither share the same roots nor have the same rights as other women or men sharing the same descent line. This form of "rootlessness" has contributed to the view of inmarrying women as "outsiders" or strangers (see chapter 6). This outside status has had many effects on women in Saklı and other communities as well. It requires women to learn and undertake unfamiliar tasks and responsibilities; it limits their ability to inherit or control property in the neighborhood and to participate in particular descent-based practices; and it restricts their ability to move about without being guarded or watched by affinal kin members. Like the Turkish diaspora in Germany, these women are expected to forgo their connections to their homeland and their "roots." For women in rural Turkey, these are the consequences of marriage and the postmarital virilocal residence practices that entail a relocation to another place. Women who move to other communities in Turkey upon marriage are said to suffer from *gurbetlik*, the state of being away from home (see also Incirlioğlu 1993, 120). In this way, the storied lives of married women in a "foreign land" parallel those of other diasporic groups, such as Turkish migrants in Germany.

There are stories of diaspora told by or about Turkish guest workers in Germany. One Turkish worker in Germany describes the difficulties of constructing a home away from home. He reveals a *gurbet* consciousness that emerges when dimensions of one culture collide with another: "We feel ourselves still to be guests. . . . If I don't feel any willingness from the other side, then I have to react as others do and isolate myself. There are two sides to (integration) . . . a majority of the German population wants nothing to do with us . . . and on our side . . . a majority does not want to change that which is familiar to them" (Kowalski and Schmidt cited in Bendix 1985, 45). The words of this worker remind me of what the Italian-born, Australian-raised writer Rosi Braidotti says about a migrant being caught in an in-between state where "the narrative of origin has the effect of destabilizing the present" (1994, 24). This in-between state bestows a sentiment of *gurbetlik*, or a longing in belonging. This sentiment is embodied in a much publicized poem, "Our Street-Sweepers in Germany," written by Fazıl Hüsnü Dağlarca. "Our Street-Sweepers in Germany" illustrates the dilemmas and cultural displacement faced by the Turkish diaspora in Germany. It is written from a perspective that draws on a story of homeland and the way a social group is displaced from one history and thrown into another:

At daybreak, fate's writing glitters on our foreheads—
That's not fate's writing, man, that's handwriting.
We can't figure it out, we have been deprived of the light of the grade
    school—
We are the sad people ruled by disgusting leaders:
We sweep the streets of foreign cities, hands filthy, hearts filthy.
My forefathers were too mighty for today and tomorrow;
I fell, I founder, a servant for foreigners now.
Only 300 years ago, we carried on our shoulders flags half the size of the
    sky
To countries whose fortresses bowed before our civilization.
Now the mouths of three children in Bünyan grow huge with hunger,
Now the eyes of four children back in Ereğli bulge with hunger:
They grab the black morsels I send out of all these darknesses.

My forefathers were too mighty for today and tomorrow;
I fell, I flounder, a servant for foreigners now.

Why stay behind? For a thousand green marks a month,
Let's go and spread out from eagle Anatolia to the face of the earth.

    Come on, let's sweep their streets,
Huge brooms, towering garbage,
Feeling no shame in the face of the crimson sun,
    Hands filthy, hearts filthy.

                                              (cited in Halman 1985, 86–87)

The above passage voices a powerful, at times crushing, awareness of the darkness and drudgery of migrant lives, of the power relations that lie in their shadows, both abroad and at home. It illustrates how memories of homeland move between the local and the global. As Gupta and Ferguson suggest, remembered places often serve as symbolic anchors of community for dispersed people, such as for immigrants "who use memory of place to construct their new lived world imaginatively" (1999b, 39). Yet past homes and places can also become distanced or blurred as migrants tread between the past and the present. In this in-between state, they encounter the powerful politics of their histories and home places from othered perspectives (see chapter 5). Their movement through time and place reminds me of what British Indian writer Salman Rushdie once said of migrants and their journeys in his book *Shame*:

All migrants leave their past behind, although some try to pack it into bundles and boxes—but on the journey something seeps out of the treasured mementoes and old photographs, until even their owners fail to recognize them, because it is the fate of the migrants to be stripped of history, to stand naked amidst the scorn of strangers upon whom they see the rich clothing, the brocades of continuity and the eyebrows of belonging. (1984, 63–64)

In addition to stories and poems within the Turkish migrant or exile literature, there are also German-produced literary and cinematic portrayals of the experiences of refugees and migrants in Germany. These differ from the authoritarian perspectives dominating the German landscape or the xenophobic speeches uttered by the conservative right-wing. One German literary work, *In die Flucht Geschlagen: Geschichten aus dem Bundesdeutschen Asyl* (Forced to Flee: Histories/Stories from West German Asylum) chronicles the experiences of refugees from eleven countries who made it to Germany (see Peck 1995, 117–118). Additionally, two low-budget films, produced by Mathias Drawe and Ragit Tuneay in Berlin, document a friendship between a Turk and a German (*Die Kunst ein Mann zu Sein*, 1989; *Der Koenig von Kreuzberg*, 1979). One film, *The King of Kreuzberg* (Kreuzberg is an immigrant Turkish neighborhood in Berlin), is assembled around the idea that the Turk is grasped sporadically by a nervous unease, a compulsion to fly or do something great. "He tries to balance on one foot, hands outstretched, back bent, hands up like flaps. This compulsion gets him into trouble if it comes while shopping, riding the subway, or making love. The urge is connected to his identity of being of the lineage of Suleiman the Great" (Fischer 1995, 143–144). It is a story that alludes to the problem of homelessness. It highlights not the stereotypes of being a Turkish immigrant but the spirit of longing in belonging. This story resembles other stories of Turkish immigrants who migrated from Bulgaria to Turkey just before World War II. It is to their lives and their stories that I would now like to turn.

NOTES

1. However, Kaplan (1998, 102) suggests that the reasons for our movements, and the terms of our participation in them, need to be historically and politically contextualized.

2. No numerical limits on workers were placed on any of these contracts until much later.

3. Not all agreements restricted the entry of dependents. For example, the agreements that Germany negotiated with Spain, Greece, Portugal, and Yugoslavia mentioned sympathetic consideration for family members, whereas the agreement between Germany and Turkey did not (see Paine 1974, 70).

4. Çinar notes that there is increasing tolerance toward dual citizenship for particular migrant groups in Germany, particularly those from Italy, the Netherlands, and Switzerland, although in 1991 of some thirty-five hundred Turkish citizens who were naturalized, only two-thirds were permitted to keep their Turkish citizenship (1994, 49–54).

5. For example, the Foreigners Law of 1990 made citizenship easier to obtain. However, the value of this reform was undermined by restrictions on dual citizenship for some groups (see Castles and Miller 1998, 242).

6. This agreement stipulated a maximum residence period of two years. However, it was subsequently cancelled two years later (see Paine 1974, 66).

7. For a detailed discussion of this migration pattern during this early period, see for example Kiray (1976), Gitmez (1979), and Kağıtçıbaşı (1985).

8. By 1965, with some 160,000 expatriates abroad, Turkey received the equivalent of nearly US$70 million in official remittances. In 1974, in the wake of new restrictions on Turkish workers going to Germany, the 750,000 Turks abroad sent home the equivalent of US$1.4 billion. By 1988 worker remittances stood at US$1.8 billion. This figure equaled the deficit of Turkey's external trade in that year (Atalık and Beeley 1993, 170).

9. For a detailed discussion of Turkish female workers in Germany during this time period, see Abadan-Unat (1982).

10. For more on "involuntary migrants" and the international regime of refugee law, see Aleinikoff (1995).

11. In the early 1970s, there emerged a decline in Turkish immigrant workers' remittances. This decline reflected the lower demand for Turkish migrant workers in Germany and the negative effects of the oil crises and the economic depression witnessed in Europe during the early 1970s. The rising unemployment that accompanied the oil crises was especially hard-felt among Turkish workers in Germany. Some of these workers were forced to return to Turkey and others lost their jobs and depended on the benefits of the German welfare state (see Doomernik 1995).

12. In 1992, in the arena of small-scale business, there were 150,000 foreigner-owned businesses in Germany, and over 20 percent of these were owned by Turks (Castles and Miller 1998, 171).

13. Much of this literature was established by authors who lived or once lived in West Germany as workers or teachers (Halman 1985, 99).

CHAPTER 5

DWELLING AND DISPERSION

In the 1930s, with the encouragement of the newly formed Turkish nation-state, ethnic Turks from Bulgaria began to emigrate to Turkey. Backed by state resettlement initiatives, a number of this diasporic group landed in the small community of Arzu in northwestern Turkey. It is in this context that I will further explore the various dimensions of resettlement. I consider this local site a focal point in the study of diaspora because here we can see how the various social, political, economic, and cultural dimensions and tensions of resettlement are played out in the lived experience of the community. The migration of members into this community created tensions for those "locals" who consider themselves attached to this place and for those whose arrival was more recent. Through ethnographic research, I explore these relations of diaspora in this specific "homeland." These relations are elaborated through tales of migration, hardship, and the group experiences of the politics of belonging. I argue that these stories of diaspora and the practices of resettlement give us insight into the social history of this place. On the margins of these stories, I will explore the various ways in which my embodied presence and ethnographic practice shape the telling of this tale.

MOBILE LIVES

Once dominated by the Ottoman Empire, the Balkan region now known as Bulgaria is home to the largest population of ethnic Turks living outside Turkey. In the centuries following the decline of the Empire, this population was the subject of many forced migrations. Following the last quarter of the nineteenth century, many thousands of ethnic Turks from northern and southeastern Bulgaria have been induced or compelled to move back to their "homelands" in Turkey. As part of the mass population interchange that took place between the Balkan War and World War I, several hundred thousand Turks left Bulgaria for Turkey. In 1925, Turkey and Bulgaria signed a convention that expedited this emigration throughout the interwar years, and remained in place until World War II ended and Bulgaria came under communist rule (see Van Hear 1998, 112). After the war, in 1950, the Bulgarian state initiated a new resettlement scheme that pressed many more ethnic Turks to emigrate to Turkey. By 1951 an estimated 150,000 ethnic Turks had left Bulgaria. A significant proportion of this group had large tracts of land in the Bulgarian countryside and engaged in tobacco and wheat farming. Most had to abandon their property altogether or sell it at a great loss. Upon their arrival in Turkey, the Turkish state provided land, seed, farm equipment, and housing, and in some cases established exclusive "immigrant" settlements. For those who left Bulgaria in 1951, a ten-year agreement struck in 1968 permitted their relatives to also come to Turkey. Approximately fifty-two thousand relatives left Bulgaria for Turkey between 1969 and 1974. The end of this agreement brought an end to Bulgarian emigration until 1989 (Van Hear 1998, 112–114).

Under a program of nationalist revival, Bulgaria instituted an assimilation campaign in 1984–1985. This campaign required ethnic Turks to adopt Slavic names. It restricted the practices of Islam, and prohibited the use of the Turkish language and the wearing of Turkish traditional clothing in public. Compliance to the campaign was reinforced by policies that delimited and directed the movements of this minority population, and entailed the issue of identity cards, the regulation of entry into paid work, and rules limiting their access to and employment in state bureaucracies and financial institutions. Resistence to these directive efforts by the ethnic Turks came in the form of organized hunger strikes and mass demonstrations. These resistence activities were largely curtailed through acts of state violence, the expulsion of activists and so-called dissidents, and the relaxation of passport regulations to encourage the further departure of ethnic Turks. The expulsion of ethnic Turks from Bulgaria to Turkey echoes in the oral histories and the stories of travel and belonging told by the Turkish immigrants in Arzu, as we will see. But the location they came to, also has a story.

A PLACE OF REMEMBERING

> To plot only "places of birth" and degrees of nativeness is to blind
> oneself to the multiplicity of attachments that people form to places
> through living in, remembering, and imagining them.
>   —L. Malkki, "The Rooting of Peoples and the
>   Territorialization of National Identity" (1999, 72)

The community of Arzu is located in northwestern Turkey in the inland region of Trakya. Arzu residents vaunt their location both in terms of its proximity to continental Europe and in terms of its association with the historical region of Thrace—the territory bounded by the Danube and Nestos Rivers and by the Black, Aegean, and Marmara Seas—from which Trakya gets its name. Today the region of Thrace is divided among the nation-states of Greece, Bulgaria, and Turkey. At the time of the establishment of the Turkish Republic, Trakya was home to a large "immigrant" population comprising peoples of Çerkez (Circassian), Artvinli, and Greek Muslim descent. Today most of the region's inhabitants consist of Pomak, Bosian, and Macedonian Muslims, and Bulgarian Turks. Trakya is noted for agriculture, particularly for the growing of sunflowers (for oil), rice, and a wide range of grain farming. Farming and agricultural activities are significant features of the region and are central in the oral histories of the place Arzu residents call their home.

Based on oral histories, the community of Arzu is said to have been first settled by four men from the same descent (kök) group about two hundred years ago. Older community residents refer to these men as either "the four kardeşler (brothers)" or "the four eski ağalar (old landlords)." The ağalar are known to have built the first and only mosque in the community. They allowed their daughters to marry men from both within and outside the village who took up residence in the ağalar households as iç güvey (uxorilocal grooms). They are remembered as having control over the fields (then owned by the state) and in preventing community residents from using them for animal pasture and subsistence farming through force of arms. Over time, most Arzu residents were compelled to work for these landlords as sharecroppers. The ağalar organized an economy of landlord–peasant labor relations, relations that persisted until the formation of the Turkish Republic in 1923 (see chapter 2).

During the years immediately following the formation of the Turkish Republic, 80 percent of Turkey's labor force was employed in agriculture and about 70 percent of the national income was derived from this employment (Birtek and Keyder 1975, 447). At this time, Arzu comprised approximately seventy farming households. Some households retained their ties to the landlord–peasant regime by working the landlord's fields for a portion of the wheat, oat, or barley harvest. Like other people in nearby communities, these sharecroppers also engaged in animal husbandry (sheep, goats, and cows) as their main economic activity, and produced butter, yogurt, and cheese for subsistence purposes. These small-scale producers relied heavily on family labor for subsistence grain farming, with surpluses sold at the market. Later residents, especially the small group of families that emigrated from Bulgaria to Arzu in the mid-1930s, never worked as sharecroppers. Upon their arrival, which we learn more about below, the

Turkish state granted them housing, land, animals, and farming inputs to encourage their involvement in subsistence farming and animal husbandry.

With the emergence of World War II in Western Europe, the Turkish economy experienced the period as a war economy. Although Turkey remained neutral in the war, national industrialization initiatives were discontinued as resources were diverted toward mobilization efforts. Even though the external European demand for foodstuffs and raw materials led to a rise in prices for Turkish exports (see Gülalp 1985, 337), agricultural production suffered setbacks as farming peasants were conscripted to military duty in large numbers. As in other parts of Turkey, in Arzu military mobilization and the confiscation of farm animals and farm goods created much hardship for local residents. Older residents recall the high rates of infant and elder deaths, malnutrition, the loss of adult males to military conscription, and the stagnation of farming. It was not until after World War II that major economic transformations in the local area began to occur.

Following the war, the Turkish state gave priority to the production of agricultural goods and minerals that were in great demand by a Europe undergoing economic recovery. At the same time, the state had also endeavored to reap the economic benefits stimulated by the Korean War.[1] Between the late 1940s and the 1950s, agricultural mechanization and new transportation routes and facilities altered social and agricultural relations in many regions of the country. For Arzu and its nearby communities, technological changes enabled the majority of residents to engage more directly in market-oriented farming. During the late 1940s, small-scale farmers started using horses in ploughing farm fields, though they still used horses to transport people and goods to and from market towns. Those who owned large amounts of land were involved in both small-scale farming and cattle breeding. One of the largest owners of farmland in Arzu recalls both the proliferation of cattle breeding and the concomitant increase in demand for seasonal laborers:

Especially between 1940–1950, there was a lot of progress made in cattle breeding. There were around two thousand five hundred sheep and about five hundred cows in the village. If there wasn't enough family members to look after the cattle, the cattle owners would hire other people for extra help. These people would come here to work as shepherds. They would usually come in groups of three to four people. My father used to hire them. He provided them with a space to stay, usually a small room in the house. Their contract was only valid for one year, beginning in November of each year. At the end of the year, if the owners were pleased with their service, they would stay on. ["How did they get paid for their work?" I ask.] Their salary was based on the number of cattle they looked after. For example, at that time, they used to get one or two cans [large tin buckets] of wheat. In those days, wheat was used in buying and selling instead of money. Wheat was more valuable than money.

During these early years, the living conditions for most other residents were especially difficult. A local male farmer, Hasan, remembers the poverty:

Our living conditions just before the 1950s were very bad, *kızım* [my daughter]. We had barely enough to look after ourselves. These were the conditions under which we grew up. It was almost impossible to wear new pants made of fabric; we always wore pants made of the type of canvas used in making tents. We always had patches on our pants. Our mothers knew how to make the patches. But, look at our children now: they wear whatever they like and they go wherever they want. Look, for example, one morning my children had said they wanted to go to the beach; they jumped in the car and went to the beach. When we were their ages, we hadn't even seen the sea. . . . Today, when people come here from other parts of the country, they feel as if they are in Germany. They say that this place is like Germany.

By the early 1950s, Arzu witnessed the introduction of tractors and an associated decline in the use of animal power. One local resident comments on the changes that occurred at the time:

In the 1940s, all of the work in the fields was done by horsepower. The fields were ploughed by using the power of horses and bulls. The farmers used to seed wheat, but they were hardly able to seed one and a half bags of wheat. In the 1950s, things began to change. Tractors were introduced. The first tractors were run with diesel fuel and were called *Forsan*. They had iron ploughs attached to them at the back. They weren't as big as the ones we have these days. Adnan Menderes [former prime minister of Turkey] introduced these tractors to the farmers. He had done a lot of useful things for the farmers. After the introduction of tractors, people began ploughing the fields that they weren't able to plough with horses. Of course, the horses weren't able to pull those heavy iron ploughs very efficiently. As a result, people's minds started to change. Once some people began to buy tractors, slowly other people began to buy them. A farmer without a tractor was not able to do anything.

According to the current *Muhtar* (village head), ten tractors and four harvesting machines were purchased by farmers, particularly by those with larger landholdings. These machines were purchased not from the market but through credit made available from the *Tarim Kredi Kooperatifleri* (TKK; Agricultural Credit Cooperatives). As one farmer said, "At that time you were able to borrow three thousand to five thousand TL [Turkish Lira] of credit from the TKK. You had to pay it back by August 1. In that way, you were able to use the money for one year. With this money people used to buy machinery, seed for the cattle, fertilizers, pesticides, or food for themselves." This new reliance on institutional credit for local farmers paralleled the situation experienced by farmers in other areas of Turkey around the same time: a 1952 survey reported that 93 percent of households owning agricultural machinery financed their purchases by credit (Keyder 1983, 42).

The mechanization of Turkish agriculture emerged alongside changes occurring in transportation. Between the late 1950s and the 1970s, a "revolution" in transportation—the advent of faster modes of transit—and in productive relations had transformed landscapes, widened mercantile and communication networks, and broadened the nature of some social relations for some groups living in Arzu and in other regions. These developments were facilitated by the state's efforts to modernize agriculture and build new infrastructures to promote agricultural production. In Arzu many new technologies and developments were introduced. These included Western farm seeds, fertilizers, and harvesting machines (the latter spawning a rental market as owners of the technology sold their services to other farmers in the area); a new irrigation system; and, later, the expansion of irrigated land. A former *Muhtar* recalls some of these changes:

For sixteen years, between 1973 to 1989, I served as the *Muhtar*. When I became the *Muhtar* in 1973 there was no electricity or drinking water in the village. So, I went and had a meeting with the people in the TEK [Turkish Electrical Industries]. We paid 125,000 TL to the TEK at the time and, in 1976, their technicians came to the village and began laying the electrical cables. In three months, TEK provided us with electricity. At the same time we also received drinking water. Drinking water was supplied to each house. Previously, you had to walk for one kilometer to get to the nearest fountain. Men, not women, used to go and get water from the fountain. Women weren't allowed to go.

During the rapid industrialization period, the landless and near landless populations in the Turkish countryside faced other changes. Some marginalized male farmers, such as Bulgarian Turks in Trakya, were forced to work as agricultural wage laborers, while others were compelled to migrate to urban centers in search of factory work. In Arzu, a number of farming families, those who did not own any land or had insufficient access to land, permanently migrated to urban centers for industrial employment. In these situations they sold whatever land they had and either sold or rented their homes to other residents in the area. Given the availability of nearby urban labor markets, some males seasonally migrated for wage work in urban factories while women (and children) stayed behind and continued to farm and to manage both household and animal husbandry activities. This migrant labor income supplemented small landholders and their households, and the once heavy reliance on animal husbandry quickly declined for most residents in Arzu.

The development of modern farming and transport technologies, and new forms of labor, commodity, and market relations, were some of the national and transnational changes that had traversed the local economy.

These interventions made Arzu a place for the intersection of hierarchically organized sets of relations. The introduction of new ideas, commodities, technologies, populations, and other transformative relations all contributed to its openings, its border crossings, and its shifts. In this way, Arzu is a place built on innumerable relations of change in terms of power, property, and production. However, one of the most significant political and cultural divisions in Arzu occurred with the arrival of Turkish immigrants from Bulgaria.

NEW ARRIVALS

Prior to World War II, massive numbers of Turkish immigrants entered Turkey from Bulgaria. Upon the forced emigration of ethnic Turks from Bulgaria to Turkey, Atatürk and his Republican People's Party developed numerous immigrant farming communities in the 1930s. Arzu was selected as a site for this form of development. Between 1935 and 1936, some forty Turkish immigrant families arrived in Arzu. They arrived at a time when each family member, under the Family Name Law of 1934, had to acquire a last name from a list of names distributed by the state. Since none of the immigrants had a "modern" last name, they were required by law to identify themselves in a new way. Their previous names consisted of a first name (e.g., Mehmet) with "oğlu" [son of] added to the end of it (e.g., Mehmetoğlu). As a consequence of the Family Name Law, it is said that three brothers in the community ended up with different last names.

After their arrival in Arzu, each family member received ten free *dönüm* (one-tenth of a hectare) of land from the Turkish state. At the time, the land given to them was already in use by "local" inhabitants. As a consequence, much land conflict developed between the two groups. Similar conflicts existed in other areas of Turkey. For example, Delaney (1991, 191) documents how the arrival of a small number of immigrants from Bulgaria created much dissension among local residents in the Anatolian community of Gökler. The state responded to this conflict by appropriating some of the community's land and forming a separate village for the immigrants. In Arzu there was no separate village formed for the new immigrants, and tensions mounted when the Turkish state gave each immigrant family one bull, one iron plough, wheat seeds for plantation, one horse carriage, and one government-built house, to encourage the immigrants to participate in farming.

As relative newcomers, the immigrants found that their claimed links to the homeland of Turkey and to their newfound home in Arzu did not override the perceived rights and the histories of local community members. Even as it became critical for them to assert their past existence as a displaced group in Bulgaria and their "sponsored" arrival by Atatürk, a new discourse of diaspora emerged as local members spoke of their new neighbors as coming from "away." Even today, Turkish immigrants in Arzu are not considered "local" by those who consider themselves rooted in the land and its history. Malkki (1999, 62) suggests that such sedentarism is not inert; it can territorialize identities. The terms of reference used to name and distinguish one group from another are indicative of this sedentarism. For example, the one group of Turks born, raised, and educated in the region are proud to call themselves *yerli* (indigenous or local peoples). The term *yerli* evokes the real tangible ties that a person or group has to a socially bounded territory. However, the *yerli* differentiate themselves from other Turkish people living in the area. They refer to the Turks from Bulgaria as *Bulgaristanlar* (Bulgarians), as people who are thought to have put down roots in a place where they do not belong. By contrast, Turkish immigrants call the "locals" *yerli* or *gacal* (natives), while referring to themselves as both Turks and *muhacir* or *goçmen* (immigrants).

Since 1935, the spatial organization of the community has been influenced by the arrival of the *muhacir*. While this spatial organization is susceptible to the play of other social differences and divisions, it is largely divided on ethnic lines. This division is apparent as one travels through the community. Approaching Arzu from the main road, there is one all-male coffee shop, one small mosque, one primary school (*ilk okul*), and one large neighborhood composed of local residents (*yerli*). These residents live in distinctly separate one-or two-story houses made of either concrete or a combination of concrete and brick. Historically, when property relations were divided along landlord–peasant lines, homes were made of *kerpiç* (mud bricks) with their roofs fabricated from wooden logs and covered with tiles. A small minority of the residents living in this neighborhood are descendants of former landlord families. They live in scattered, two-story homes with imposing balconies and with garages designed to house automobiles and agricultural machinery. Some of these houses either sit alone in the open country or are strung out along both sides of the road. Most houses in the upper part of the community (*yukarı*), are surrounded by vast agricultural lands located in the back or to the side of household buildings. During the late summer months the fields are blanketed with bright, long-stemmed sunflowers.

Past this neighborhood, there is a smaller neighborhood located near the bottom of the main road overlooking a *mera*, a field of open grassland used as sheep pasture. This lower part of the community (*aşağı*) consists of the group of *muhacir* who live in single-story houses that are closer together. Far from being concealed, the neighborhood is conspicuous, as it complicates the "local" sense of time. It evokes an image of modernity, of diffuse plans to administer and individualize populations. Its image sets it apart from the rest of the community. It is one of Atatürk's "modern" housing projects organized to accommodate new "national" arrivals. The *muhacir* live in a landscape of white-washed mud-brick houses that have fenced backyards. These backyards are reserved for small-scale sheep raising, *ça-maşirhane* (laundry houses), *bahçe* (gardens), chicken pens, and outdoor toilets. The hand-painted "for sale" signs mark the fronts of a select number of empty, desolate-looking, abandoned homes that have their windows boarded and their front doors bolted with large locks. The former inhabitants of these homes have permanently migrated for work in urban centers and have sold their land and aim to sell their homes to neighbors or relatives. While I was living in Arzu, two families were forced to sell their homes to pay for the healthcare costs of a sick family member. Those who remain in the area pride themselves on getting through the war years, the "scarcity period" of the early 1940s when food was short and many went hungry. These and other similar hardships are revealed in the stories people tell of their lives in Arzu. The ethnographic fields of these oral stories, and their transformation into written text, need to be made clear.

STORIES IN ETHNOGRAPHIC FIELDS

There are many different kinds of oral and life stories: stories traced with feet and eyes, stories unfolded through listening or reading, stories passed down from one family to another, and stories told about personal lives in transition. These stories have authors and listeners and they comprise reflections of sites, events, or relations. But these storied fields involve more than knowing who is doing the telling, what is being told, and where the telling is taking place. There is a relationship formed between the teller and the listener, between telling the tale and hearing it (Razack 1996, 165)[2] or writing it. In this way, researchers themselves play a mediating role in the creation of the stories that appear in their ethnographic productions.

Ethnographic fields are the social vehicles within which stories emerge and are transformed. Our presence as researchers plays a critical role in mediating the dialogue between ourselves and others. The very fact of being physically present can bring to the surface the social experiences of people's complex habits, sentiments, and cultural inventories as they might express them in daily life stories. In *A Passion for Difference*, Moore suggests that our presence, as researchers, gives meaning to the ontology of intersubjective and embodied experience and the manner in which social interactions are embraced in concrete relations of space and time (1994, 3). She brings to the forefront the need to acknowledge how we are involved in producing and constructing the stories that are told to us that later appear in our ethnographic writings. This means that processes of selecting, editing, or translating are neither transparent activities (Phillips 1996; Göçek and Balaghi 1994) nor necessarily separate from colonial structures of cultural domination (Su 1999, 38). It is useful to make these processes translucent, even though they may raise questions about the ways in which *we* are involved in articulating other people's stories and lives *for* them. On this point, I am reminded by Rey Chow's analysis of the way in which some Chinese elite intellectuals, when addressing the international public, speak "for" less privileged members of their home culture as a "Maoist version of orientalism" (1993, 14).

As a researcher I often find myself at the crossroads of the many intersecting social, cultural, economic, and political relations. Through my embodied presence and participation in these relations I have come to learn of the varied experiences that shape people's storied lives. This engagement is not straightforward, and my trajectory is not linear. More like following a flow than pursuing a ready-made route, I make myself vulnerable to the various branches and forks that pass through diverse stories, commentaries, and conversations and find it necessary to negotiate, at every intersection, the course to follow. Before these stories can be articulated, I need to make clear, both to myself and to readers, how my role as a researcher enters into and shapes the creation of storied knowledge (see Stacey 1991, 115). Let me begin by first saying that I enter into and travel with the stories that are presented in this chapter and in other chapters. These stories are articulations of particular women and men whom I chose to speak with and who agreed to speak with me in the ethnographic fields of Arzu.

In as much as I would have liked to share in and listen to many life stories in Arzu, it is not an easy task to ask someone to reveal their life unless one is willing to go through a process of passing. In Arzu, trust is a prerequisite for extended contact with individuals who are not considered either close kin or neighbors. It is a kind of trust, or as they would say *güvenlik*, that assures them that the information they give me won't be used against them. Many residents believed that I had the opportunity to come into contact with many different "trustworthy and untrustworthy" people. This contact could potentially mean that I would have the chance to circulate information from my informationally saturated status as both researcher and visitor. So, to gain their trust, I abided, for the most, by the prevailing rules of public *adet* (custom) and lived similar to the way that some community members lived. I regularly visited their homes, expressed to them aspects of my work and family life, and answered their questions of my *araştırma* (research) and what immediate use it could be to them or to others, if of any use at all. This initiation process offered a way to begin the cycle of reciprocity, of visiting each other and of sharing and exchanging thoughts and stories. This cycle often translated into a form of valued cooperation between people, especially among the women from both the "upper" and the "lower" parts of Arzu.[3] This initiation process opened the possibility for them to reveal their stories. This way of assembling social communication reflects just one of the many negotiated elements involved in the process of ethnographic research and writing. This negotiation process suggests that researchers are both producers in the text and producers of the text.[4]

The stories included in the next section of this chapter are the views of those who migrated from Bulgaria to northwestern Turkey and who were variously rooted in and uprooted from their cultural homeland. For those who returned, this homeland was not a place for which they held any cultural or historical claims to sovereignty. Although the homeland was a landscape of historical memory for them, it did not offer them tangible feelings of belonging. Their state of diaspora was a consequence of their ever present migrant status and their perceived otherness. Their stories of diaspora reveal these relations. They are articulated in their own words— words that are a product of our encounter at the margins of our worlds and that neither of us can rightly claim as property. These stories belong to a place and a time that is difficult to identify, since it was formed in the passage of our conversation and the reflections on passage that were formed therein.

My enthusiastic interest in their storied histories, migrations, and movements often made these Turkish immigrants feel like their place in history mattered, especially since someone equally outside expressed an interest in listening. In many ways these stories are much more important for the *muhacir* to tell, since by telling them they are able to invoke their own participation in historical processes. Telling stories of the past also places the storytellers in a position of knowing and experiencing certain events that other, younger family members have not experienced but are nevertheless eager to listen to and learn from. Within this storied world, the past becomes increasingly important for Turkish immigrants from Bulgaria, whose perspective on the present is less than certain. This uncertainty is a result of their migrant status and their mixed feelings of belonging in a community now considered as their *only* home. The emphasis on the past parallels Ganguly's study of members of the Indian diaspora in the United States. In this study, she argues that the past becomes increasingly significant for people whose view on the present is variable as an effect of implemented displacement. As she states, "the stories people tell about their pasts have more to do with the continuing shoring up of self-understanding than with historical 'truths' " (1992, 29–30). In the case of the *muhacir*, however, their stories reveal dimensions of the social and political histories that influence both their personal and their family lives. Their storied histories remain an ever present part of their relations with others.

My interest in their storied histories somehow made them feel, as they would say, *rahat* (comfortable) to tell of incidences that they would rather not repeat too often. However, I was made aware that not all visitors to Arzu could be privy to their worlds and their words. Upon my first visit to Arzu in 1996, I was told about a survey team of Turkish researchers who visited Arzu for "three consecutive days" in 1994. I was informed that these researchers were from "some university in Istanbul," though the community residents couldn't remember their names or institutional affiliation.

The researchers asked the residents numerous questions about their migration experiences, household composition, and work patterns. They held papers and pens in their hands and spoke like they wanted to be heard in a way that Arzu residents were unaccustomed to. One group of men had told me that they had answered the researchers' questions but merely told them lies. Another group of women had told me that they were not permitted by their husbands to speak to them.

At first, the story of the research team made me think about the value of participant-observation and interpersonal understanding, and the level of familiarity, dialogue, and exchange that one needs to develop to interact meaningfully with individuals and groups in field research sites. It was made clear to me that the survey team did not approach research in this way. The story also made me recall my ethnographic research experience in rural Turkey in the late 1980s, not only its interpersonal and communicative elements but also its politics: the politics of obtaining permission to do the research from regional and local authorities; the politics of being a "stranger," of listening to other people's stories, of asking questions, of visiting some groups more than others, of self-presentation, and of traveling and being seen, the latter of which is often a delicate issue for female researchers in rural Turkey. More than this, the story of the survey team served as a constant reminder of the ethical issues endemic to field research, of the sometimes exploitative and hierarchical relations of conventional research and classical interview methods. Although I was aware of the dilemmas, the inequalities, and the conflicts that besiege even the most self-reflexive relationships between researchers and their collaborators, it was my hope that my embodied presence—as a Western-trained researcher with some Turkish heritage—would not be portrayed as an antagonist encounter or an unwelcomed intrusion into their social relationships.[5] Perhaps the concerns that I had about being temporarily part of their lives was the story's intended, pedagogical effect. I could only hope that my role as a student of their stories, and my interest in their storied histories, would be accepted on their terms. For after all, I was merely a *misafir*, a guest, in their historically situated and fragmented lives.[6]

In the following pages, I introduce a series of life stories as a basis for understanding aspects of migrancy and mobilization in Arzu. Issues of diaspora and resettlement practices figure prominently in these stories, and they alert us to the ways that settlements both abroad and at home are cut across by various forms of interchange. For the most part, these are stories told to me by Hacer Teyze,[7] a woman whom I visited regularly throughout my stay. She lives in the "lower" neighborhood of Arzu with her married son, daughter-in-law, and grandchildren.

STORIES OF DIASPORA

Hacer Teyze's oral life stories are moving, provocative, and educational. Her life experiences express varied upheavals, across many spatial settings, through the temporal modalities of past, present, and future. Like other life stories, her stories rarely flow smoothly and directly from one theme to another. There are pauses, hesitations, bodily gestures, and gaps that not only distinguish her stories from others, but also make them open to invitations and allow other thoughts to enter. These stories often seem to lose their sense of place and time. When oral life stories are transformed into written text (as I have done with Hacer Teyze's), the punctuations, silences, and expressions of speech are displaced. As Ricoeur (1979) says, once an oral production becomes a written product, its openness as dialogue is lost. It is here that I, like other researchers (see chapter 3), encounter the problems associated with translating and retelling. This leads some researchers to question the ethics of ethnographic practices and skills, the constructedness of the voices of storytellers, and the role of ethnographic authorship in cultural productions.[8] My transformation of Hacer Teyze's oral stories into written text confronts the same dilemmas; these stories remain caught in the world of my text. Against the backdrop of the issues associated with textually mediated productions, I present Hacer Teyze's stories in a written form for two main reasons. Following feminist work on storied lives (e.g., Dossa 1999; Phillips 1998; Abu-Lughod 1993; Cole 1991), I believe that her articulations are a way of emphasizing the relevance of this woman's thought and not just mine. Also, her stories, despite my editorial transcription and translation, act as an important pedagogical medium that stirs the depths of diaspora.

My purpose in presenting Hacer Teyze's stories is to enable her expressions to describe the circumstances of her migration from Bulgaria to Turkey and to provide her with the opportunity to tell the story of her arrival in Arzu and the events that followed in the way she likes to tell it. Her storied memories draw upon recorded and unrecorded events as well as things heard and overheard. They give us a sense of the complex and the ironic spaces of order, practices of sharing, domains of work, and an understanding of locality shaped by contestations within and between regional and national settings. However, her life stories do not flow from one point in time to another or from one topic to another. Her stories move through the past, the present, and the future as if these conventional temporal boundaries were limits to overcome and thresholds to be crossed in the movement of her understanding.

As a listener of and a participant in Hacer Teyze's storytelling, I would sometimes interject by asking questions and making comments. Sometimes these interruptions would encourage her to recall some events in greater detail or to link particular events to other events. Also, as a translater and transformer of her recorded oral stories into written words, and all the complexities that such work entails, I occasionally offer—on the margins of her storytelling—a further elaboration of the ideas and issues that she raises. This is not only because her story necessitates that I listen carefully, but also because it inspires me to write from another angle and to think of other moments and movements of translation, of transformation. In this way, I am involved in stretching her storytelling along other routes and at the various places where our thoughts cross and intersect.

Like the stories presented in other chapters, Hacer Teyze's stories, sayings, and passages propel themselves into other networks and relations. For me, this dimension of mobility makes these stories dynamic and leads to other stories that could be told. Hacer Teyze is a dynamic storyteller. I wish that every one of her sentences could be written out as a single line of words running into the distance—gathering up memories, picking up or rerouting other ideas, sayings, and anecdotes along the way—so that it would be clear that sentences are like a branching stream rather than being neatly fixed in a row.

A Journey Home

One of Hacer Teyze's stories recollects her experiences of migration from Bulgaria to Turkey. In it she highlights the particular and the mundane:

We came to Tekirdağ [the largest town on the Marmara coast] as immigrants. I was twelve years old at that time. . . . The *gavur*, I would like to call them this [reference here is to the Bulgarian nationals as "non-Muslims"], began to kill the Turks, and because of this we were afraid. Our fathers were afraid and they decided to come here. The Bulgarians used to come and collect the men from the houses and kill them. That's why we came here, *kızım* [referring to me as "my daughter"]. We were afraid. In the beginning we were able to go out—to the market, to visit our relatives and friends—but later on we were unable to go anywhere. We all had Turkish neighbors, but we were unable to visit them. Once the Bulgarians started to behave badly to us, we began to be afraid. My parents had five children. They said: "we should take these children to Turkey. After that I don't care what happens to them there, but it is a better place than here." [Was anyone killed among your relatives, neighbors, or friends, I ask.] Nobody was killed among our relatives, but we heard of several cases in our neighborhood. They [the Bulgarians] were afraid of my grandfather so they didn't touch us. But, my grandfather was worried that they were going to kill us, so he sold all of his land for one-tenth of the price and came to Turkey. We barely made it to Istanbul and we had no money left. Later Atatürk sent us to Tekirdağ, then from there we came to Hayrabolu [a community], and from there we were spread to several neighboring villages. We set up a farming business here. The government gave each person ten *dönüm* of land. They gave us lots of wheat too and we finished that wheat in two years. The government gave one bull to each family. They also gave one to my *gelin* [her daughter-in-law]. So what people did was they got together and used those two bulls to plough the fields. The government gave us houses; they built houses for us. Some of houses that are being demolished right now are the houses built by Atatürk. These houses aren't concrete buildings, they are made by using mud and mud-brick. Murat's [her brother-in-law] house is one of them. It has been many years since Atatürk passed away [1938]. I was young then; now I am seventy-six years old. He was so nice: he looked after us, he built us houses, he gave us bulls. After receiving all those things, the people began to work in the fields and their lives improved slowly.

From Hacer Teyze's opening migrant story, there is a strong sense of diaspora that is invoked by her and her family's experience of political hardship and social and economical displacement in Bulgaria. This sense of diaspora calls forth a connection, and an eventual relocation, to a "homeland." Yet the processes of leaving one place for another, of belonging in some place, always seem tarnished with the possibilities of truly getting in and fitting in. In this regard, as a Turkish immigrant who once lived in another land and was compelled to return "home," Hacer Teyze has alerted us to how the meaning of coming home took on a new sense of belonging. From an astute historical standpoint, she has hinted at how returning "home" mobilized different patterns of migration. Her story does not stop here; it takes us in a direction that points to some of the ways that resettlement practices bring about the changing configurations of social relations:

We knew Turkish when we lived in Bulgaria. But they [the Bulgarians] wanted us to learn Bulgarian, and later on they were successful at that. Most of the people who immigrated recently [around the late 1980s] know Bulgarian. When we came to this village . . . this neighborhood [where she lives now] was full of *muhacir*. The upper part of the neighborhood was full of *yerli*. In this neighborhood there were two long rows of immigrant houses. Once the children living in these houses grew up, their families couldn't look after them. There weren't enough jobs for them. But if these children had been given fields, they would have stayed here. Look [pointing to her neighbors across the street], they have five children and the children don't even have one *dönüm* of ploughed land. The same thing will happen to these children: they will leave. We had a tractor. When Neriman's husband [Hacer Teyze's son] was in the army, my other son would plough the fields with his father. . . . I remember something about my son. When it was midnight, my husband would take the tractor out, and my son would grab the gun and sit next to him. He was nine years old; imagine, he was nine years old at the time. They would plough the fields at nighttime when everybody was sleeping. My son used to say that he could see a man in the field next to his father. His father would tell him that there was no man in the field: it was the tractor. He would see the lights of the tractor from a distance and thought that it was a man. He was nine years old.

They [her husband and sons] worked in the fields, thanks to god. But if the government hadn't given the land to us, the land that we ploughed, then we could not have stayed here. . . . Look, so many young people have left; their numbers have decreased. Most of them didn't work in the fields because there wasn't enough land. Whatever was left from their fathers, they didn't work hard enough to make it more. Whenever they marry, whenever they leave here, ten *dönüm* of land will be left. [I ask, "Could you tell me more about your work in the fields back then?"]. We used to work in the fields, we harvested manually by using "reaping hooks." We used to go back and forth between the fields and the house. I can't believe now how we were able to do that. We used to go to the fields, work, come back home, prepare meals, and take them to the fields. I used to take my children back home, feed them, and make them sleep. Later I used to return to the field again. I had five children. I had two brothers and I was the only girl. If we had more land, we would have been more crowded. When we separated, each of us only got ten *dönüm* of land. We also have ten to twenty *dönüm* of registered land. The rest is not registered but nobody is trying to take it from us. We have one hundred and fifty *dönüm* of land in total: fifty *dönüm* of land is hers [referring to her daughter-in-law], fifty *dönüm* is Kazim's [her second son], and my son in Istanbul has fifty *dönüm* of land. . . . This land is separate from the land that I received from my parents. Whatever we had was divided into three. I have separately fifteen *dönüm* of land. Kazim rents out this land and I live with the money I get from it. It is not enough, but it is better than nothing. My daughters also help me out. They send me money.

I am intrigued by Hacer Teyze's recollection of her early experiences of household farming, of her knowledge of networks of landed property and ownership, and of her thoughts on the problems associated with having insufficient land to sustain a resettled and growing population. What strikes me about her recollection of property relations is that it makes one think of arriving in a new settlement and acquiring things in the processes of settlement. It also marks the apprehensive interstices of going, of doing things, and of moving elsewhere. As a term, "settlement" tends to imply an established order of things that is found within its borders, its geography, its history.[9] However, settling in a place is a profoundly unsettling social activity. In Hacer Teyze's words:

Well, we were very poor in the 1930s. The *yerli* were also poor; they were very poor. But, when the tractors were introduced [1950s], they bought them. They had gold and they sold the gold to purchase a tractor. Once they bought the tractor, they never stopped working in the fields. The *yerli* didn't want us to work in the fields, but through gun force we [the *muhacir*] were able to plough some fields, to work in the fields. They were more free to work in the fields. They used to work in the morning, in the afternoon, and in the evening. They were free to work in the fields at any time. We had to struggle a lot to be able to work in the fields.

Settling in a place may have an intensely unsettling effect on people's daily lives, although it does not mean that one cannot or is unwilling to create those necessary strong and reassuring relations that allow one to function in a place called home.

Border Intensities

In conjunction with other life stories dealing with issues of resettlement practices, Hacer Teyze's story forces me to question the concept of settlement in order to lose the points of arrival, the positions of permanency, and the privileged relations of staying that are imbricated in it. No settlement is ever complete. It is always in a process of settling, unsettling, and resettling. To focus on what these practices can do, what they can produce or mobilize, what they blend and connect with, would produce a stronger, dynamic account of settlement issues than simply focusing on what a settlement is and what it consists of. Practices of settlement seek and provoke other relations. They cross other boundaries, migrate alongside other settlements, and produce change. This seems to convey the point made by Jansen; in studying "a world of movement" for displaced inhabitants in the former Yugoslavia, she argues that there are at least two levels of movement: "people are traveling (physically and mentally), but even when they stay at home they can find themselves displaced, for borders are traveling as well" (1998, 98). These mobile relations make it possible to understand not only why a settlement is never fully bounded, but also why it is always going through processes of deterritorialization, of intensity and in-betweenness (Probyn 1996). Here I am reminded of Hacer Teyze's earlier discussion of living in the immigrant section of Arzu, a site of constant junctures of belonging in and between social relations. Through my conversations with Hacer Teyze and other members in the neighborhood, I have come to understand that their place in this juncture of in-betweenness is perceived in a number of different ways: from the incessant way that Turkish immigrants from Bulgaria are perpetually in-between two settlements, cultures, and histories, to the ways that their *goçmen* neighborhood is assumed by the "locals" to be separate from the rest of the community. As a consequence of their in-between location, they have been the target of a mass of othering practices and linguistic naming conventions that differentiate them from the locals. Also, their location in the space of in-betweenness, in the place they have come to in the hopes of a change toward a better life, facilitated feelings of homelessness at home. These feelings emerged in a series of telling incidents that highlight the workings of power and the challenges of belonging. In Hacer Teyze's words:

Once our sons had to stay in the police station under police control for no reason, no one understood why. Another time, Osman [a relative] was also taken to the police station by the *yerli*. This incident happened sometime after Kazim returned back from the army, god rest him. When he heard about the incident, he took two sacks of flour to the police station and gave it to the police. It was then that the police let Osman go. Another time, my other son, Neriman's husband, had a field of thirty *dönüm*. He was growing wheat in the field at that time. But the *yerli* released the cows into his field and the cows destroyed most of the wheat. My son called the government inspectors. They came and analyzed the damage and the situation. We sued the *yerli* and the trial lasted four years. It took four years to come up with a decision. His father, god rest him, used to say: "They will come up with a decision this winter, but I won't be able to see it." We won the case. The result was in our favor; we gained our land again. There was wheat in the field, but we couldn't harvest it. How could we harvest it? Kazim said, "We will apply to the government to give us money. Whatever the government decides, they will convert the wheat into money." Anyway, we went there [to the government office]. One of the people who worked there said, "Why did you come here?" He was my relative from my home town whose father had died. I said, "They were going to give us money." He said, "What money?" I said, "I don't know, the government was supposed to give us money." He said that there was nothing like that available. But, they ended up paying us the wheat's worth. They gave us the field too; we had gained the field. I don't know why the *yerli* didn't want us.

Not only were there struggles over landownership and land access, but there was also a loss of family land as a consequence of a particular form of marriage practice. As Hacer Teyze recalled:

There were eight to nine people living in our house. After we came here, my grand-father died in less than a year. One year after him, my grandmother died. The government didn't give them any land. If they had been given land, we would have had more land. And, we would have had more land if it wasn't for my brother. My brother had kidnapped a girl [referring to the practice of elopement]. Actually, he kidnapped a girl who was engaged. In order to keep the girl's family quiet, we sold his share of the land and gave the money to them. At that time, we used to plough the fields manually; we used to harvest manually through the use of reaping hooks. After we harvested the wheat, we used to grind it to obtain flour. But we would get very low yields from the fields; the yields weren't as high as they are now. We were able to sell only a very small portion of it. ["The yield was so low that, after feeding yourselves, there was little left to sell on the market?" I asked.] Yes. At that time, there was no pesticides and fertilizers. We used to have low sunflower yields. If you had good productive soil, you had good yields too.

At this point in our conversation I was eager to learn more about how her brother had "kidnapped a girl" and why people resorted to practices of "kidnapping" at that time. In Turkey, *kız kaçirma* (lit., "girl kidnapping") refers to elopement and rarely involves the actual abduction of women. Nevertheless, this practice works against the moral values of arranged marriages and parental sanctions, values I had already learned about during my one-year stay (1988–1989) in a northwestern, mountainous community (Saklı) located in the province of Zonguldak.[10] During my research in Arzu in 1996, I discovered that *kız kaçirma* was practiced by the *muhacir* as a way for families to avoid paying bride price, especially among the poorest families. The poorest families in Arzu are the *muhacir*. They own the least amount of land, have limited access to expensive farming technology, and are unable to send their children to trade schools or institutes and colleges of higher learning. Hacer Teyze tells us more about this marriage practice in relation to bride price:

Well, if you had the time and the money to marry, you got married. If you didn't have time and the money, then they would kidnap you and you wouldn't have any wedding ceremony. My wedding was an arranged *evlilik* [marriage]. We moved to this village and they [her husband's family] moved to this village. They came to our house one day and asked permission from my father to have their son marry me. My parents gave their permission. He [her husband] had seen me in the minibus and liked me; he wanted to marry me. He was a *çoban* [shepherd]. . . . His family wanted him to marry me and my parents agreed. My parents asked for *başlık* [bride price payments]. It was money worth something back then, but now it isn't worth much. Anyway, they [my husband's family] didn't buy me much stuff. So, my father decided to marry me with someone else instead. I escaped from home in order to marry my husband. . . . I didn't ask for a *düğün* [wedding] because I didn't have any *çeyiz* [trousseau, usually consisting of scarves, hand-knitted sweaters and socks, handmade lace, embroidered bed linens, etc.]. How was I supposed to have a wedding ceremony? Both sides [the bride and groom's families] couldn't afford any of the arrangements. Both sides were poor. My parents tried to marry me with the son of a rich family. They were from Muzurupulu [another village]. His [the potential groom's] sister was staying with Rasim's and Suleyman's families here. I didn't want to marry him; instead I married my current husband. And with him, I faced both poverty and prosperity. ["Where did you move after you got married?" I asked.] We moved into the houses where Aysel is living with her family now. They used to be our houses. I married Murat's brother; Murat, as you know, is my brother-in-law. He was living in the house at the time and so was my mother-in-law and father-in-law.

I knew Hacer Teyze's brother-in-law, Murat Amca.[11] He was younger than Hacer Teyze and operated a coffee shop below my residence—a place reserved for government officials, resident doctors and nurses, and other itinerant folk like me. He would always call in the morning or in the early evening to find out if I or my research assistant and friend, Selma, needed anything. Even though we would thank him for calling and said we didn't, he would often arrange for a youngster to bring us hot tea from the coffee shop.

Murat Amca, like Hacer Teyze, is a Turkish immigrant from Bulgaria. He lives alone in a small house that is adjacent to his son's. Over the course of time that I lived in Arzu, he was one of the first people who talked candidly and openly about the ethnic conflicts in the community prior to World War II:

When we first came here, the carriages were pulled by either a donkey or a cow. People weren't as well off as they are now. The houses here were all small, their ceilings were low. I remember my father telling us about the time when the Greeks were defeated in the War of Independence [1919–1923] and had to leave the country. On their way out, they destroyed all the houses and the barns. Nothing was left in the villages. When we [the *muhacir*] came here, the *yerli* were rebuilding the whole village. Well, they were just out of a war! Even my father used to tell us that they weren't able to stay in the village during the war; they had to hide in safe places outside the village. They were able to return to the village at nighttime, maybe at daytime, I don't quite remember. My father was young at that time when he told us these stories. He used to say that the Greek army was able to do whatever they wanted. They were able to take over the houses and the land. If the *yerli* had cattle, they used to kill and eat them. When we came here, the *yerli* were just beginning to normalize their lives; they were working hard to improve their living conditions. At the time, we lived with them until our houses, houses built by Atatürk, were complete. Every local family had to host one immigrant family until their house was complete. The *yerli* learned a lot from us. When we arrived, they were using wooden ploughs in the fields. For the first time they had seen the iron ploughs that we were using. So they began ploughing the fields with iron ploughs. Also, the *yerli* used to build their houses without a proper framework. They used to put wooden logs on the roof and cover it with tiles. They used to have big chimneys on the roofs of their houses. When we came, we brought with us stoves that were made from tins with added pipes. Our houses were always warm. The stoves were very efficient. We set an example for the *yerli*.

His recollections bear similarity to Hacer Teyze's thoughts on the lives of immigrants and their modes of belonging in Arzu, although she recalls other events that took place during the 1930s and 1940s:

Well, some of the immigrants who came here didn't stay here for long. They left and went to other places. Lots of immigrants came, but some of them didn't stay here long because they weren't able to find work. Once Atatürk died [November 1938], things began to change. Things weren't like they used to be. The *yerli* didn't want us to use the land that the government had given us. They insisted on saying that all the land was theirs, even though they never legally owned that land. As a result of that, some immigrants didn't stay here for long. But, we had plenty of land and it provided income for two to three families. ["Is this why you and other members of your family have continued to stay here?" I asked.] Yes, we had enough land to stay here but we always had to protect it and ourselves from the locals. We had the toughest days when we first came here. When we first arrived, we had nothing and my parents had hard times when they were raising us. We worked very hard. We used to look after our brothers and sisters when my mother was working in the fields. Human beings are very strong, they don't die from sadness and hard work. We had good times too. In the evenings we would get together in someone's house to sing songs, religious songs. That is how we would spend our time. We didn't have stereos and televisions; we had to sing the songs by ourselves. There wasn't any tea in those days, so we used to serve corn instead. We would even serve corn during *Mevlut* [a religious ceremony of commemoration]. You cook the corn kernels in water. It is very delicious. They don't organize *Mevlut*s a lot these days like they used to. In the old days, they used to organize them a lot; one week I used to organize it, the next week someone else used to organize it. They would usually serve dinner during the *Mevlut*. They would read forty *yasin* [a section of the Koran] during the *Mevlut*.

Before I left Hacer Teyze's house one day, she insisted on telling me a story that she thought would be of interest to me. It speaks to issues of generation and gender in historical and contemporary context. It is a story that reflects some of the many discussions we had about giving birth and raising children in Arzu:

You know that when we first came here, we faced poverty for a long time. But as time went on, we worked hard, and now we have prospered. We did sheep breeding in small amounts. We sold sheep, milk, and lamb. We used to breed and sell *koç* [ram]. As you know, this is how we made our living. . . . We sold to people in the village and to people from other villages. They used to come from other villages to buy from us. I'll never forget, I was pregnant and was expecting a girl. My husband had gone to [a nearby community] to sell sheep and I gave birth before he came back. Before he went, I said to him, "I am going to die by the time you come back." He said, "You won't die, nothing will happen to you." I had birth pains and I said to him, "Where are you going, I might die." He said, "You won't die, God knows when that will happen." By the time he returned, I had already given birth. I gave birth nine times, all of them at home without a doctor. I always had an experienced local woman with me. I made nine children, but only five of them lived. My first child died after forty days of his birth. After one year, I had Kazim, he lived. One year after that, I had a girl, she also died after forty days of her birth. You never know what God has decided for you. After that I had my daughter, who is in Istanbul now; she also lived. Kazim and her are both alive. Meanwhile, my father-in-law had died and, around the same time, I had another son, Necip. So one of my children died, the next one lived, and the next one died again; that is how it happened. Thanks to God, they are all fine. I don't want to see any of their sadness; that is my *özlem* [wish, desire] from God. Now, all my grandchildren have grown up; they are all together now. My first grandchild married, the rest are all bachelors. I don't know if I will live long enough to attend their marriages.

These last two passages, similar to earlier ones, underscore the themes related to the ethnic Turks in Bulgaria, their arrival into a new place, and the struggles of diaspora that still confront them in their homeland. These themes are most especially revealed in the expressive stories told by Hacer Teyze. From within the terrain of these stories, the *muhacir*'s resettlement practices are shown to be infused with hope and despair, a longing in belonging, and wishes and responsibilities. In the context of both the present and the past, the *muhacir*, like the Turkish migrants in Germany, live in an in-between place. It is a place that often conjures feelings of homelessness at home and experiences of transit and transition. The following chapter focuses on another form of transit and transition, one involving a distinct group of married women who have resettled in Arzu and engaged in practices of resettlement that question and unravel various relations of power.

NOTES

1. See Ahmad (1993) for a detailed discussion of this historical period of intense industrialization.

2. I am reminded of the concerns that Razack raises when refugee women in Canada tell their stories in courts and before judges, juries, and lawyers. As she says, "the stories are being told to make a particular point and they are being heard in a particular way. It will not be possible to squeeze all the realities of daily life into this framework; some realities are distorted to the point of their being unrecognizable. Indeed, storytelling as a methodology in the context of law can lead very quickly into dichotomies and generalizations that make it difficult to describe the intersections of race, class, gender and disability" (1996, 167).

3. In many ways, it was far less complicated to visit women in their homes than to visit men in their homes without their wives present. This is due in part to the political dimensions associated with gender and space relations. Conducting oral histories with men required that their wives, or other female members within the community, be present. As discussed in chapter 6, there is much moral scrutiny around women being in contact with "unrelated" men, and this applies to me when I am in their world, although perhaps less intensely.

4. This discussion raises the broader issue of the relationship between the author of the text and the author in the text. As Moore claims, this is not a direct and straightforward relationship. It is not straightforward because one author is the imaginary self of the other author. And, because of this, the relationship between authors "is fictive in the sense that it is arbitrary and symbolic, set up in language and culturally inscribed" (1994, 117).

5. For similar and other related concerns in ethnographic research, see Bridgman, Cole, and Howard-Bobiwash (1999); Cole (1992); and Stacey (1991).

6. The story of the survey team also made me think about my research agenda in the community and to be responsive to how local residents wanted to participate in the research process. I am reminded here of an important question ("Who are we for them?") that Celia Rothenburg (1999) posed to herself when she was engaged in field research in the West Bank.

7. In kinship terminology, the term *teyze* refers to one's mother's sister (MZ), and this term is used to address one's MZ. However, in daily interactions, the term *teyze* is used to address older women. For example, girls and boys would refer to me as Suzan Teyze. It is a term utilized to denote closeness and familiarity. In contrast, the term *hala* is used to refer to one's father's sister (FZ). It is also reserved to address those to whom one wishes to show respect. Community members, like other members in different communities in Turkey (see Delaney 1991; Ilcan 1994), perceive their relationship to their mother (and her relatives) differently than their relationship to their father (and his relatives).

8. See Salazar's discussion (1991) on the tensions related to autobiographies and ethnographic productions.

9. For a comparable discussion on the theme of settlement or territorialization, see Rodríguez (1994).

10. See my earlier work (1994) for more on the practice of *kız kaçirma*.

11. The term *amca* is used to address one's father's brother (FB). This term, however, also addresses men with whom one does not share a kinship relation. For example, older men are addressed as *amca* by younger women, men, and children.

CHAPTER 6 _____

SUBVERSIVE MOVEMENTS

In this chapter I focus on the ways in which women in Arzu challenge their place of dwelling in the disciplinary space of the household.[1] Specifically, what I am interested in are the subversive practices that transform these spaces. The conventional understanding of women's place in the "developing" world views households as a site of gender politics where relations of hierarchy, authority, and power are brought to bear on women and shape them into "subjects" of this social environment. At the same time, however, there has been little research on how women reappropriate these social spaces. What I argue here is that women are not simply subjects of the household space, its timetables, and its routines, but that they create, through their collective and recollective strategies, space and time for themselves. Through these processes—not always known in advance or self-present to others—women reconstitute their lives outside of institutional habits and arrangements.

In light of these issues, I explore how rural women, through their provisioning of space and time, devise alternative relations of belonging that are both political and communal. I begin by setting out the shifting, theoretical boundaries that have encouraged me to think not only about the movement of our ideas but also about the attractions of movement for women. Primarily through ethnographic illustrations from Arzu, I examine the conditions under which women live in the settled space of households: the site of duty that often regulates women's time because the caring, feeding, and reproduction of household members (as well as the production and consumption of household goods) presuppose a place for such activities. From here, I show how women shift away from regulated activities and authoritarian relations and create a marginal space from which they are able to speak the unspoken, tell stories, and invoke change. I suggest that this shift calls for the invention of particular relations, where other geographies and forms of agency can be engendered. In this transgressive context, women's mobile or nomadic encounters are shown to produce new perceptions of and possibilities for material life. This is especially so for those who enter into communities and households from the "outside" and establish mobile coalitions with one another. This nomadic theme is depicted through women's everyday practices and their diverse stories of displacement.

SHIFTING GROUNDS

Most research on women and space in the rural "Middle East" conceives the "private" sphere of the household as a site of women's seclusion and oppression, a place that controls women's identity, mobility, and sexuality. There is no doubt that the spatial and temporal organization of these rural household economies positions particular women in marginal ways. This is due, in part, to endogamous marriage practices, virilocal residence and property inheritance patterns, and the moral codes of behavior that circumscribe stringent gender divisions of labor.[2] However, in line with new feminist insights against conventional or dominant depictions of women or gender (e.g., Aucoin 2000; Melman 1996; Khouri 1996; Blunt and Rose 1994), it is important to bear in mind that women are capable of changing the disciplinary regime of the household and its settled ways. I think here of Abu-Lughod's concern (1993) with the generalizations that have been made about Middle Eastern women and how these have produced a homogeneous, coherent, and timeless portrayal of women's experiences and of "culture" (see chapter 3). By working against generalizations, by "writing against culture," Abu-Lughod undoes the "typicality" of women's lives so often produced in social scientific accounts. She accomplishes this by illustrating how Awlad 'Ali women challenge common interpretations of "Bedouin culture" through the textual technique of storytelling. In her words, "telling stories . . . could be a powerful tool for unsettling the culture concept and subverting the process of 'othering' it entailed" (1993, 13). Similar to this critical ethnographic style, and following some of the feminist reflections of poststructuralism and postcolonialism, I explore how the concept of nomadism is useful for challenging the rigid, institutional views of life and for understanding rural women's movements and their moments of sociality. These are subversive movements that unsettle the practices of settlement.[3]

The concept of nomadism is a metaphorical style of thinking that cultivates and elaborates "new frameworks, new images, new modes of thought." As analysts, it allows us to move through and migrate across established boundaries without burning bridges. It is a move against conventionally bound frameworks (Braidotti 1994) and "outsider" perspectives. These perspectives are often associated with the sedentary presumptions of modern and colonial constructions of culture. Unlike imperial and colonial discourses—especially their spatial and temporal delineations of power and dependence upon fixed views of "other" people and places—nomadism is another mode for thinking about the movement of our thoughts, for setting into motion universalized ideas, peoples, and places, and for considering the specific "circuits of travel" (Ong 1995, 351). It permits one to question what is taken for granted and what is already in "place." It does more than merely unsettle "one's own thinking habits" (Minh-ha 1991, 21). It encourages a change in our habits of thinking and a revitalization of the way in which we analyze space and time relations. In this way, it involves moving away from targeting women as victims of hierarchical and disciplinary spaces to a focus on recognizing women's ability to displace relatively binding structures and their affiliated practices. This notion of displacing routine ideas or activities, what I call a *nomadic disposition*, relinquishes the nostalgia for permanence. It thrives to cross boundaries and denaturalize stable identities, habits, and practices. This concept parallels Minh-ha's "strategies of displacement" and the way these strategies unsettle the world of compartmentalization and the systems of ties generated (1991, 23). It also resonates with Probyn's "outside belonging," a term used to instill the movement associated with the wishing to belong, particularly the manner in which one's productive desire to belong places us "on the outside" and provides immense political possibilities (1996, 9).

Perhaps more important, nomadism is a kind of critical awareness that resists settling into socially coded modes of thought and behavior (Braidotti 1994, 5). People's unsettling endeavors, such as women's activities of movement and contest, signal a minority group's critical awareness about being active and bringing about change. It is an awareness that does not dwell in the past or accept the rigidity of hierarchical relations and chronologically regulated time. In this regard, nomadism coincides with bell hooks' "politics of location" (1990). This location involves interrupting one's place and creating a space of "radical openness," a new location from which to articulate a critical response to domination and a new sense of the world. Both of these concepts propel and set into motion different possibilities for thinking about one's position and relationships with others. In counterdistinction to inhabitation, nomadism is a way of understanding the process of transformation. It is ultimately about *changing places*: the capacity to displace one's habitat and routine habits.

Settling In: Disciplinary Spaces and Socially Directed Time

It is well acknowledged that disciplinary spaces—such as the social institutions of correction and training, schools, workshops, households, and so forth—prescribe gestures and command bodies. These spaces confine people to act, behave, or work in particular ways according to chronologically regulated time and labor divisions. As common sites for individualizing and directing groups of people according to a homogeneous orderliness, people here are not born into their places: they need to be trained, socialized, and controlled in specific ways.[4] For example, in patrilocally extended households, senior elders have considerable authority over other household members. This means that young adults, especially daughters and inmarrying women, are, and have been, subject to distinct forms of corporeal inscription and social regulation (e.g., Moghadam 1993). In this way, these spaces are marked with a certain mode of detailed political investment of the body, where the art of discipline proceeds from the distribution of individuals in an "enclosure," a place different from all others and relatively closed in upon itself (Foucault 1979, 139–148). Designed and organized for specific duties and practices, relative enclosures establish individual habits, lifestyles, and movements.

Disciplinary spaces settle people into particular ways of living. They divide and combine activities into unified motion. Settling into a particular place accommodates socially coded modes of thought and behavior, permitting likely encounters and sources of interaction, experience, and knowledge. For example, in some rural Middle Eastern households, women are placed in hierarchical positions based upon age, kin, and authority relations (e.g., Moghadam 1993; Sirman 1991). This settling potentially situates them in positions of unpaid domestic and farm work and envelops them into spaces of duty, of perpetual and endlessly repeatable tasks that have increasingly little recognition[5] in comparison to paid work positions (see Erman 1997, 264). Especially relevant in this context are the numerous stories that describe how former peasant women in Arzu have become "confined to the home" (*evlerine kapandı kaldılar*) since the development of mechanized farming in the 1950s. One older, male farmer clarifies the changing role of women during the process of modernization:

I bought my first tractor in 1952 and my first harvesting machine in 1953. With the introduction of these machines in the area, there was not even enough work left to be done for men, let alone women. With the use of harvesting machines, the need for sickles was reduced dramatically. . . . After mechanization, women had less to do and their life became more comfortable. They used to bake their own bread and do the laundry manually. Now they have stoves and washing machines. Now they have fridges. Before that, they didn't have them. They now have vacuum cleaners. In the early days, they didn't have carpets. Also, these pull-out beds are new;

they weren't available in the old days. They didn't have heaters either; instead, they had ovens in which they would burn coal or wood to provide heat. Today, women's work is easy. They now have water heaters: you press a button and it provides hot water. Now they have drinking water at home; whereas in the old days you had to transport buckets of water from the community fountain.

The modernization of farming in the region of Trakya, especially the introduction of labor-saving farm technologies, the importation of Western, commercial seeds and fertilizers, and the increasing market demand for agricultural products, has produced new divisions based upon social class. It has also restructured lifestyles and social arrangements, and reordered the movements of people (see chapter 5). Within this format of change, new spatial conceptions of gender and work relations have emerged. For example, most *modern* men in Arzu are now considered to have acquired the necessary knowledge, technology, and outlook to meet the demands associated with agricultural production, market economies, and commercial exchange relations. Different from the past, they rarely engage in subsistence farming activities. Nor do they spend much of their time at home during the planting and harvesting seasons.[6] Rather, their time has been increasingly geared toward the market through their engagement in an elaborate social network of buying and selling relations in the case of the trade of agricultural commodities; labor exchanges in the case of the local labor market; and banks and less formal financial "houses" in the case of the circulation of capital. With the increased production of exchangeable goods (along with their transport, delivery, and sale), the extension of town markets, and the expansion of capitalism, the spaces for men now extend far beyond Arzu's borders and work sites. Not surprisingly, men leave their marks in places where women often do not. They leave their impressions with town bankers, coffee shop owners, and itinerant merchants. They leave their signatures on property deeds, bank notes, and transport licenses. The territories, architectures, and sites that they occupy, and the routine activities that they engage in, vary from those of most women.

Since the mechanization of farming and the increasing absorption of men in formal market relations, *modern* women in Arzu are now thought to have indolent bodies that just *"sit at home."* In this context, "sitting" (*oturma*) denotes relaxation or comfort, and the verb "to sit" (*oturmak*) means to live or dwell in a place with others. Interestingly, the activity of sitting is perceived in many ways, ranging from the way in which women are now thought to be comfortably settled in their homes to the way in which they, in comparison to men, are thought to be freed from the land. Sitting has now come to mean the opposite of work or the *other* of work. The use of the term "sitting," especially in reference to what women do, is employed by older generations to indicate women's changed routine-habits. Its use not only expunges women's household work and the record of their movements but also establishes a fixed image of what women do in households. That is, for women to be known just to sit not only conjures and controls a present and a future but implies that they are positioned, that they are immobile, that they have an abode. It is only in settled places that women are seen to have a particular place to inhabit. This is where their apparent sitting-habits are considered to liberate them from the constraints of contemporary agricultural demands.

This traditional view of settlement suffers from a number of shortcomings and lacunae. I would like to interrupt this timeless portrayal of women's sitting-habits with another, more processual and mobile, image of settlement. When I think of women's sitting-habits I think about their household work routines, where their daily childcare, domestic, and productive activities establish rhythms, regulate the cycles of repetition, and thus order and partition time. The daily chores—of planning and preparing meals, taking care of children, husbands, and sometimes the elderly, the weekly tasks of preparing butter, cheese, and yogurt, making bread, washing laundry, housecleaning, and the seasonal demands of garden work, household wall plastering (sıva), indoor painting, and labor-intensive farm work (such as hoeing)—are the main activities performed by women in Arzu throughout the year. However, these activities may be performed with changing frequency and intensity, depending on alterations in household size, the use of household technologies, and the presence of inmarrying women. In any case, it is women's movements through household space, exemplified by their planned work routines, that command them. There is *the* time to wash, cook, feed, sew, and mend, and to tend to household members' demands and expectations. Like Marx's conception of labor-time, the household work routine quantifies time; it portions out the time for certain duties and therefore classifies, estimates, and ranks temporality.[7] In this way, the activities that occur in the settled space of households fix the meaning of time: time is planned, ordered, and calculated. Women's time is occupied by the spatial routines of the household.

In addition to time and mobility constraints, the obligations imposed on women by older household members (especially on young brides) have disciplinary outcomes. From the very beginning, and upon her arrival in the extended household,[8] a newly married woman is generally not permitted to visit her natal family until forty days after her wedding. It is assumed that after this period a bride (*gelin*) will be settled into her new abode (see also Delaney 1994, 161). If she does not already know how to present herself in front of her newly acquired relatives and neighbors, she is taught to show respect to those older than her, instructed to talk and dress appropriately in front of guests, and trained to sit properly. She is also expected to do various household chores, and this work is often concluded with an examination by a mother-in-law who will judge the level of her performance and authorize the necessary improvements. However, while

this form of power surveys, supervises, and observes a *gelin*'s bodily behavior and her interactions with others, such technologies of power rarely
go unnoticed. A young, newly married woman from the "lower" part of
Arzu (see chapter 5) commented on her sense of spatiality: "I had a very
hard time adjusting to the lifestyle here and I am still trying to adjust. This
society is very different from the one I came from. I tell you this house is
like an *açık hapishane* [open air prison]." Nevertheless, a well-disciplined
bride is considered to be a hard worker, a polite and attentive host in the
company of elders and guests, a "good" wife, and a household's mark of
distinction: she reveals to others the household members' good judgment
in finding a suitable bride for their son (and also for them) and for bestow-
ing the appropriate bride price (*başlık*).[9]

In the agricultural areas of Trakya marked by the mechanization of farming and the modernization of household economies, the household is typically a place organized for the unpaid work of women and the caring of
the bodies of men and children (feeding, clothing, and replenishing activities). However, this does not mean that women do not transform the settled
domain of the household and its timely duties; nor does it mean that this
is the only site of women's activity. Household spaces are much more complex when we consider women's relationships to them. As Sirman says, "all
social structures open up particular spaces of operation for socially positioned individuals, [and] we should investigate what this space consists of
for women and what women do within this space, as well as the means
available to them for enlarging its boundaries" (1991, 201).

Unsettling: Women's Space and Time

> The marginalized position of the exile, at the very least, provides the
> exile with the perspectives of an outsider, the kinds of perspective that
> enable one to see the loopholes and flaws of the system in ways that
> those inside the system cannot.
> —E. Grosz, "Judaism and Exile" (1993, 69)

Settled spaces can be displaced through people's alternative practices of
space. They can give way to new spaces that create new images, new experiences, and new modes of perception.[10] In this process of transformation, one may not have to go far to change one's place or to change places
(see Braidotti 1994, 5). In fact, rural women in Turkey and elsewhere have
been known to occupy the household not simply as a central site of domestic duty, of social and generational reproduction, but as a nomadic
space for socializing and participating in female gatherings, neighborly visits, and informational exchanges. Unlike settled spaces, nomadic spaces do
not divide or disseminate populations in a network of relations; they are
not cellular or rank-ordered, since there is no partitioning of places for

individuals and no individualized places. They do not have the rules of
conduct that define for us the meaning of "knowing how to act" or "how
to respond" as found in the disciplinary spaces of households. These sites
offer the potential for creating alternative relations of belonging, since there
is no one state of affairs given completely, no one set of principles to follow,
and no one way to act. It is in these marginal spaces that place seems to
matter most while the place located in the center of things grows ever so
predictable and familiar (see Stewart 1996, 42). The most central of locations can be transformed into places where there is no hierarchy of order
and no regulated routines.

As in other areas of the rural Middle East and Mediterranean, in rural
Turkey it is common for a woman to leave her natal household upon marriage and move to her husband's parents' home.[11] This woman is known
as a *gelin* ("the one who comes"). Except for unmarried women, and the
occasional *kız kaçirma*,[12] every woman is a *gelin*. However, the term *gelin*
furnishes a subtle negativism; it not only highlights the foreignness of
women who marry into the community but draws attention to their flight
of passage and minority status. Women, more than any other group, are
expected to abandon their homeland and former identity and to enter into
a new place of habitation upon marriage. In fact, married women are said
to have come from the "outside" (see also Delaney 1991). I remember when
I first heard an older woman identify both herself and her daughters-in-
law as *yabanci* (outsiders, strangers), a term referring to those who origi-
nate from another community, who are descended from other ancestors,
and who are distinguished from the indigenous, local people (*yerli.*) This
comment struck me as I imagined over one-half of the community population belonging on the boundaries of a place. It also alerted me to the
stories of spatiality and the tropes of proximity and distance that continually weave relations among people, places, and things.

What does it mean to come from the outside, to be a stranger? I posed
this question to myself and to others when the opportunity arose. Is it a
position of transmigration, of signaling a capacity to be transferred from
one place to another, to be subjected to the twists and turns of social life,
to be marked by a sense of loss or separation from a homeland? I recollect
the story that Aysel told about a flock of wild (*yaban*) sheep who were
labeled *yabanci* due to their "history of lacking a home environment and
of being fed in the forest by a lazy *çoban* [shepherd]." I recall the tales
about the groups of *çingene* ("gypsies") that traveled to the region to work
as farm laborers (for a few weeks every year during the hoeing and planting
seasons) and lived in plastic tents positioned on the side of the main road
and isolated from nearby communities. I was warned to stay away from
them because "they steal." "They are wanderers," I was informed, "who
never stay for long." This statement left me wondering about the large
number of rural migrants who settled on the periphery of Istanbul in shanty

town houses called *gecekondu*s ("built overnight"): were they outsiders too? The numerous experiences and stories of being an outsider were all too familiar to me, for I too was an outsider: a Western-trained researcher, with dual citizenship and Turkish "roots," who moved from a permanent place of residence to a temporary abode in another "homeland." From the perspective of those who consider themselves conventionally naturalized (native, provincial), I had a denaturalized status: I lacked a direct kinship connection to community residents and did not belong to the community from the beginning.[13] However, while this outside/outsider status has been and continues to be applied to women (and to the *muhacir* more generally) in largely sedentary ways, it has a means of not standing still: it tracks the places where one has been, it sketches one's territorial crossings, and it charts one's historical departure and arrival. We could say then that an outsider's disposition delineates an inventory of traces, of passages, of movements: it is nomadic. It compels, even as it rearranges, the relations that it interrupts. As Grosz suggests, "the outside or the exterior is what both enables and resists the movements of territorialization and deterritorialization" (1995, 131).

Rather than reifying women's outsidedness in tropes of tragedy and isolation or depicting women as the victimized "other," perhaps we can unsettle this view by looking at the ways in which women politicize and make use of this imposed outsider status (cf. Abu-Lughod 1993, 116–121). I see it as essential to understand how women displace their patterns of regulated activities and move out of the disciplinary domain in which they find themselves working and living most of the time. This is an understanding that works toward exploring how women bring about change through time and space configurations. Such a disposition emphasizes the permeability of boundaries and the potential to change places. There is a critical, perhaps a wishful thinking side to my position: that there must be ways for women to deterritorialize those spaces in which they find themselves settled in order to challenge their patterns and practices of settlement. This position, as Braidotti would say, "is the intense desire to go on trespassing, transgressing" (1994, 36). The vital, though unsettling, value of this position is that it makes one increasingly aware of the construction of gendered culture, the creation of spatial boundaries, and the rhythms and ordering of time.

The ability to transform the household's disciplinary space into a nomadic one is influenced by a particular conception of time quite different from modern time. Modern time is directed and planned. It is dominated by those spaces where things are produced and invested: time recorded on measuring instruments, time spent working, time assessed in terms of value, money, and the production of commodities (Lefebvre 1991, 95–96). However, a time that is not administered or managed is one that allows women to displace the household and its habitual routines. Minh-ha suggests that "displacement involves the invention of new forms of subjectivities, of pleasures, of intensities, of relationships" (1991, 19). I would add that in order to engage in this process of change, an undirected conception of time is necessary. When undirected time trespasses on social spaces (as opposed to the control of time by movements in "modern" spaces), then there is the potential for women to have visions and wishes and to tell stories. Such reflections on social life are not only politically valuable but are also mobile: they incorporate a notion of the future and a distancing of the past. As I illustrate below, women populate the marginal space of the household. This is a space of alternative relations of belonging, similar to Probyn's "outside belonging" (1996), that challenges regulated positions and designates a profound manner of shared nomadism for women. Their contacts with their female neighbors—in the form of economic cooperation, informational exchanges on domestic decisionmaking, local healing remedies, bride searches and marriage negotiations, as well as their discussions on household politics and conflicts (especially those between women and their in-laws)—highlight their sharing of outside differences. Especially when they engage in activities that have little to do with being settled or under the rule of authority figures, they do things differently; they unfold autobiographical histories, tell stories, and disappear from household duties and time-bound habits for a while.

As a visiting pattern common in other regions of Turkey,[14] the *kabul günü* ("reception day") is an event that ruptures everyday routines, makes no claim to consistency, and gives rise to forms of movement. The *kabul günü* (locally referred to as simply *günü*) is a good example of a female gathering that takes place in the nomadic space of households and involves activities separate from those that characterize the settled space of households. It is a well-organized event. Once a host receives permission from her husband to hold such an affair, she is then responsible for inviting individual women to her home on the designated reception day. These invited guests are typically young married women from varied social-class groupings within Arzu. Such visits generally take place in a designated host's household about twice a month (especially during the spring and summer months) and include between twenty and forty women (Ilcan 1998a). More important, however, the reception day creates a space to challenge those master narratives that "speak a war of positions" (Stewart 1996, 97) and locate women in traditional reproductive and caring roles. It is a time for women to talk openly about their lives as *gelin* and to highlight the issues and struggles that they face as women who have entered the community from the outside. It is for these reasons that men and mothers-in-law are not invited to such events, for they are often perceived as the source of tension and conflict.

Women's stories during reception-day events reflect an untiring distaste for settlement. The themes of these stories range from issues of marriage, family life, and restricted spatial mobility to those of education, economics, and community politics. An important thread running through these stories is the way in which women tell them from another point of view or from a nomadic disposition. To clarify the use of this concept in this particular field, the term "nomadic" refers to an alternative mode of thinking and awareness that allows women to question common cultural assumptions and sedentary views of life. By disposition, I am not only referring to women's outside/outsider status, which certainly uproots them as well as grants them a particular character, but to their ability to challenge their place of settlement. It is for these reasons that these stories are worthy of reproducing here, if only to get a sense of women's "comings and goings."

Reception days are not impromptu affairs; they are transformative events. They take place in a nonauthoritarian space and in an untimely manner. They are infused with critical accounts of the past, the present, and the future, of stories pertinent to women's lives. On one occasion a newly married woman, who had a grade-five education and was disenchanted that she had not progressed higher, spoke of gender as a site of struggle and of the injustice that families impose on their female children. Her story not only moves uninterruptedly from one vantage point to another, from outside to inside, and vice versa, but it also elaborates a description of the territories that are crossed in a woman's journey. It also alerts us to a conception of the "way things are managed" and "the way things could be managed":

There are no limits for men. More opportunities are provided to men and there aren't enough opportunities given to women. I always argue about this point with my father. He rented a car and took my brother to school every day. He could have done the same thing for us [her three sisters]; at least he could have sent us to *orta okul* [middle school], but he didn't. If you ask him why, he will say, "Even if my daughters earned a higher education, their husbands wouldn't let them work." So, because he would have to spend all that money on us for nothing, he thinks women's education is pointless. There are a few women here who finished university but they aren't allowed to work. My uncle's daughter finished a two-year university program, and she was the district governor's secretary. Later on she got married and they [her husband and his parents] wouldn't let her work. They said to her, "Stay at home and do the housework; later on you will have a baby, and you will look after your children instead of hiring a babysitter." So, they don't allow her to work.

Like this woman's story, other storied recollections emphasize women in transit and their experience of what it means to be displaced, or what Minh-ha calls "living in-between regimens of truth" (1991, 21). Hayriye, born at the beginning of the 1970s and raised in a farming community several hours from Arzu by car, told the story of her marriage to a local man, her move to his parents' house, and the difficulties of living "here." She began by recounting her life as a farm girl, the close friends she had back home, and her love for her natal family, whom she rarely sees now. She highlighted the intricacies of her engagement and arranged marriage to a man whom she described as having completed both high school and the mandatory military service, a rare accomplishment in the eyes of most people given that he had come from a poor family who did not own much farmland or technology. After I asked her if she would talk about her move to Arzu, her storied recollection turned to her difficulties of adjusting to a new place, a new family, a new way of life. With confidence in her voice, she said: "When women marry and come here, they leave their families and their friends behind. Sometimes it is many days later, even weeks later, when you find out about the things that have happened back home. My family is far away from here. As you know I can't just go and visit them. Last year I visited my family once during *bayram* [religious holiday]. . . . I am obliged to be here: to look after our house, to prepare the food, to feed the animals, to help my mother-in-law." After the other women joined in the conversation, telling their own experiences of moving to and settling in the community, Hayriye posed the question:

What do I have here? Of course, I do have my children and my husband, but I cannot do the things that I would like to do. I cannot always go where I want without first getting permission (*izin*). Before I can visit my relatives or even visit my neighbors, I must ask my husband and his parents. . . . This life is not what I had really expected. It was not my wish to live in the countryside with my in-laws or to do what they demand from me. But, what choice do I have now? . . . Still, I have made a life for myself here. I guess you could say that I have adjusted. I have friends, I have my neighbors. . . . I have wishes too. When I was a little girl my mother used to tell us that "our wishes are our possessions" (*tek varlığımız dilek-lerimiz*).

"What kinds of things do you hope for?" I asked. With much enthusiasm, she replied by saying that "someday, I wish to move to [a nearby town] and have our own house, with a garden, like we have here. . . . I would like my children to have a high school education and maybe go to university. *İnşallah* [if God wills]."

Shared by many women, these alternative views of another place and another time interrupt an attachment to settled ways and evoke new visions. The yearning for a different kind of life or the telling of a wish foregrounds the notion of dislocation. Each is a form of reflection on the temporality of existence conveyed through a present translation of an experience in the past.[15] Through their ability to seize what is taken for granted and unravel it to new and varying levels, women are able to think differently and recognize other ways in which they can live outside their routine lives. This is an important feature of women's shared stories and experiences in nondisciplinary spaces. Having similar household positions

and perceptions of relocation and adjustment, their outside/outsider standing is, and has been, critical for invoking the positive effects of reception
gatherings, especially the development of a collective awareness of their
relations with others.

Women's shared reflections in gatherings less formal than those of reception days also express a dynamic mode of questioning and rethinking
issues of positionality. In fact, the most common and near-daily gatherings
take place when women visit their female neighbors, usually during the
day—and between meal times—when their husbands and fathers-in-law are
laboring in the fields, purchasing goods from the town market, or participating in activities within the all-male coffee house. In these gatherings, the
disciplinary, household space becomes transformed into a nomadic one, a
place where women exchange information, share ideas, and tell numerous
stories of their settled lives, restricted travels, and past experiences. During
one household gathering, an older woman, reflecting an historical knowledge of shifting grounds, recounts and recasts how women's travels from
one home to another required justification. Her story also reveals that "sitting" is not a woman's choice:

In the old days, women weren't able to go out and visit friends. When I first came
here [forty-five years ago], women used to look outside from their doorsteps. They
weren't able to see one woman on the street. Women were always in the garden.
If they really had to go out and visit someone, they used to wear a veil and cover
themselves. Only then, in the company of other people, could they go out, pay the
visit, and come back again in the company of the same people. Only the old people
(büyükler) in the family visited neighbors, and if you wanted to go with them, you
had to follow them. We always had to sit at home.

In remembering the stories that her mother-in-law told her, a younger
women echoed similar sentiments of the past in the context of the changing
present. Her story, only partially recapped here, locates women's agency in
shifts and transitions. It highlights the complexity of women's place in a
specific time and space:

In the past, women weren't able to go out much. Now we are able to go out. For
example, in the old days it was harder to go and visit someone. You first had to
finish your housework and then maybe you could go and visit your friend once
during the winter. Women were only able to visit one family during the winter, but
they visited their neighbors frequently. My mother-in-law used to tell me that people didn't have the habit of visiting each other like they do now; now, a man can
see his close friends at the coffee shop and their wives can see each other at home.
Years ago, women . . . couldn't visit each other because they had to spend most of
their time working, working in the fields. . . . They weren't even able to do their
needlework; they had to come home from the fields, cook the dinner, get water
from the fountain, do the laundry, and make bread at night after spending the day

in the field. The following morning, they would take their bread with them and go to the fields.

No matter how minute, mundane, or meticulous, these stories are mobile: they disrupt the boundaries of women's routine lives, they move in and out of history, and they compel connections among women.[16] Moreover, they are shaped and influenced by a concept of undirected time that is distinguishable but not separable from space. As Bakhtin suggests, "time, as it were, thickens, takes on flesh, becomes artistically visible; likewise, space becomes charged and responsible to the movements of time, plot and history" (1981, 84). The importance of this time, the time to tell stories, occurs at those points when women's positions and locations in settled spaces become interrupted. Undirected time not only marks change but also is about change. The trespassing of undirected time over space envelopes a fluid and fragmented sense of space where women can challenge the practices of their settlement. It is for this reason that the expressing of new visions and the telling of wishes are so significant: they are not tied to a present but are constantly on the move.

Being within and between sets of social relations can enable rural women to traverse disciplinary boundaries. Although women are the ones who have been brought in from the "outside," they are the ones who have also brought with them new questions and who have dealt with their displacement in ways that introduce change. Over the past several decades, especially since the modernization of farming, women are seen as the ones responsible for slowly challenging "Ottoman" women's dress and the restricted movements of women. In the face of authoritarian regimes, arranged marriages, and "forced" migration, women, as I have shown, do question the norms and confront the practices of their settlement. They have struggled to develop ties with others by establishing cooperative female networks: farm-work groups, reception-day assemblies, neighborhood gatherings. As an important feat for women, these networks permit them to exchange private information on the economic affairs of and conflicting demands within their households. They also permit them to question, through storytelling, their rank within the hierarchical order of things and to develop different ways of envisioning their lives with others in a process of social change. These changes range from breaking down the barriers of women's household isolation to devising new strategies and ways of knowing that permit women to assess and negotiate the forms of control imposed upon them. Women's lived materiality of being "outsiders in the inside" has in effect politicized their disposition. Through their shared activities in unsettled places, women are able to produce alternative accounts of their belonging, for they are the ones who have the great capacity to import new qualities and strategies into community life. Indeed, they serve to remind us of other, perhaps not so visible, dimensions of dwelling. It would be erroneous to assume, then, that women merely operate within institutional frameworks and moral value systems without interrupting them.

The metaphors of travel and migrancy have been used by analysts to convey a sense of process, flow, and transversality in the spatiality of social life and to cross the meanings of center and margin, inside and outside, private and public. The conventional views of women's space and time have emerged within those universal frameworks such as modernization, disciplinary regimes, and the institutionalization of social life. However, in order for us as analysts to highlight the diffuseness of women's place and politics, we need to be able to deal with the constraints of those settled and tradition-bound perspectives that have a habit of keeping us in our place, of encouraging us to stay focused on those dominant social structures without ever recognizing their openings. By ignoring these constraints, we face betraying people's struggles in the specific ways in which they practice and live them. This is why, in Kirby's words, "we cannot afford to naturalize the boundary, though we must analyze boundaries that have been naturalized in order to break down their rigidity. We cannot afford to reify the distinction between 'inside' and 'outside,' though, in formulating a politics, we cannot abandon either space but must continually traverse the difference" (1993, 189). We should therefore not underestimate the numerous effects that materialize when marginalized groups change places and create alternative relations of belonging. These relations challenge the practices of settlement. As I have suggested in this chapter, it is in unsettled spaces that women's politics of storytelling forge a critical awareness among women. In this regard, we need to reconsider how disciplinary spaces are lived and how they may be transformed by nonauthoritarian, mobile practices.

NOTES

1. This chapter is a very close version of a previously published essay titled "Challenging Settlement: Women's Culture of Dis-placement" (Ilcan 1998b). It is included in this book because it deals directly with the subject matter of my project and it inspired me to continue my research and writing on the cultural politics of settlement in broader terms.

2. See Moghadam (1993, 104–109), Ghorayshi (1998), and Ilcan (1996a; 1996b) for more extensive discussions on these issues in specific areas of the Middle East.

3. These practices often have a reserved place in the popular discussions of "the" Islamic Middle East.

4. See Ilcan (1998a) for more on disciplinary and marginal spaces.

5. See Grosz (1995) on women and dwelling.

6. Only on formal occasions of an engagement or a marriage will men stay home in the evening to participate. It is considered morally appropriate for a man

to spend his working hours, and his communal affairs, with other men outside the household (see Ilcan 1998a).

7. See Grossberg (1996, 179) on how the timetable controls movements through space.

8. Household membership in this region, as well as in other areas of Turkey, is generally based on kinship through marriage and descent.

9. Disciplinary strategies characterize the domain of family households not only at the community level but also at the level of the nation-state. This is evident in state policies and civil codes pertaining to matters of family, gender, and property relations in Turkey (see N. Arat 1996, 403; Y. Arat 1996, 29). The government's monitoring of parental and conjugal relations in claims of citizenship and its regulation of license marriages, property inheritance, divorce, and child custody procedures are among the most controlling tactics used to authorize aspects of family life, sexuality, and reproduction.

10. Nikolas Rose makes an insightful point with regard to governable spaces. In his words, "Governable spaces are not fabricated counter to experience; they make new kinds of experience possible, produce new modes of perception, invest percepts with affects, with dangers and opportunities, with saliences and attractions" (1999, 32).

11. See Aucoin (2000) for a discussion on the ways in which women are drawn into ranked relationships through marriage and virilocal residence practices in Western Fiji.

12. The literal translation of the term *kız kaçirma* is "girl kidnapping." It mainly applies to couples who have "run away" to get married without parental approval. See also chapter 5.

13. See Simmel (1950, 402–408) for a discussion on the phenomenon of the stranger as a condition and symbol of social relations.

14. For a discussion on this visiting pattern in cities and towns of Turkey, see: Aswad (1974) and Benedict (1974). For visiting patterns in other areas of the Middle East, such as in Yemen, see Meneley (2000).

15. See Bell (1994) on dreaming, time, and dislocation.

16. See Hanson and Pratt (1995) for an interesting discussion on women's "mobility stories" in contemporary Worcester, Massachusetts.

CONCLUSION: MOBILE RELATIONS

Counter to viewing social relations through the lens of rigid institutions, fixed territories, rooted communities, and established groupings, I have focused on movement and have analyzed social relations in the field of their dispersion, transition, and displacement. This book has examined various ways in which social and cultural relations cross territorial bounds and go beyond ready-made frameworks and institutional dependencies. These relations are characterized by their links to mobility and their ongoing practices of movement, dislocation, and relocation. The focus on mobile relations expresses a concern for the transit of people, ideas, and images, and the implications these movements have for nation-building, ethnographic practice, dwelling, and diaspora. The pursuit of the diverse flows of these mobile relations brings with it an understanding of the uneven and complex social practices of settlement. These practices cannot be reduced to centralist tendencies, concentrations of power, stable structures, or images of social order. Instead, settlement practices are directly linked to the strategies and configurations of mobilization that establish and transform them.

The twentieth century can be distinguished by the expanding numbers of refugees, migrant workers, and immigrants who have been displaced from national, regional, or ethnic locations. A focus on the mobility and mobilization of peoples, populations, and places gives rise to new inquiries about the ties people have to their dwellings, and the kinds of enduring settlement practices constituted for those on the move. For those who travel from one place to another, who dwell in the borderlands, or who are considered out of place in their abode, their practices may be permeated with ambiguity, but they nevertheless accommodate themselves to this instability. Transnational communities, diasporas, and migratory networks are current examples that provide insight into the tensions and risks of movement confronted by those who are compelled to leave one home for another or those for whom belonging has been superseded by longing. The tension between movement and dwelling confronts populations that are resettled in places that are no longer self-perpetuating, autonomous, or clearly bounded (if they ever were) because they have been mobilized by other worldwide forces. There are also risks (political, economic, spiritual) associated with the journey of longing to belong, with following a path that stretches toward, or terminates in, places less attractive than others and with the recollection of places abandoned and other paths forgone. However, these tensions and risks are not principally located within the geographical borders and temporal confines of a given society; instead, they are dispersed across regions, networks, and the contours of global and local experiences.

Twentieth-century nation-building efforts provide insight into the challenges faced by newly constructed populations and their dispersion in numerous paths and practices of settlement and resettlement. Nation-building is a journey of longing to belong in a settlement process that compels a movement from one home to another. For nation-builders, belonging to a nation is the supreme form of belonging, one that should surpass, displace, and subsume all other forms, such as that of the family or local community. Belonging to a nation is heralded not as a choice but as a secure path to follow now and in the future. This path to follow is often described as producing a sense of being with and for the nation, even though any attachment to the nation comes in all its styles and symbols of location and displacement. As Ignatieff reminds us, "the nationalist claim is that full belonging, the warm sensation that people understand not merely what you say but what you mean, can come only when you are among your own people in your native land" (1993, 10). As outlined in chapter 2, nation-building takes the form of a migrant nationalism that tells the story of people passing through history. It lingers between home and homelessness and involves dimensions of unsettling and resettling groups of people, ideas, and symbols. In the case of nation-building in the early modern period of Turkey, I showed that its primary aim was to unsettle the traditional practices of central cultural representations in the movement from an empire to a nation. In this unsettling process, the nation-state assigned new codes, signs, and symbols to those who carried the nation along in its transit and to those who were slow in following the same path. For the journey to the modern world, some new codes of conduct were introduced to separate formal religion from the state and others were designed to develop new linguistic systems, regimes of time, and styles of dress. These codes of conduct required a new pedagogical style and a new way of circulating the signs of modernity both to the masses and to the West. The mobilization of nationalist gender and family relations was central to the strategy of recoding the Turkish nation-state and was particularly high on the state's agenda. The modern woman and the modern man were two new characters that the Turkish modernity project scripted and conscripted in its movement. The former spanned the gulf between the past and the future. She was distanced from the past but projected into the future through her recognition in the development of new family codes, particularly through the adoption of the Swiss Civil Code. In contrast, the new modern man was scripted along the lines of his bodily presentation. The bodies of men, their distribution and habits, could neither go unchanged nor go unnoticed. They needed to become a book of instruction and a lesson to be learned if the nation-state was to present itself to its people and their neighbors with an appropriate air and manner upon its arrival in the new homeland. Overall, the nation-state memorialized movement, speed, and circulation. The changes brought about through the Kemalist reform movement hinged on traversing the distance and difference between an empire and a modern Turkey at infinite speed. Displacing and replacing both a population and its territory relied heavily on the symbolic resources it was able to mobilize for the passage. While the violence of this migration to modernity was of a different order than that experienced by other diasporic groups in terms of the means used in forced exiles and expulsions, the Turkish nation-building movement has nevertheless stood as another example of the many massive cultural movements that we have witnessed during the twentieth century.

Through my interest in nation-building movements and its settlement practices, I have come to appreciate the need to develop methodological practices that do not root "cultures" in space and time but emphasize the mobile dimensions of cultural production. These dimensions of cultural production range from the transformation of worlds and words, the interacting forms of transformation and movement, to the poetics and politics of ethnographic moments and ethnographic lives. In chapter 3, I illustrated the interrelations of habitation and movement in contemporary ethnography. In drawing upon current debates in the field of cultural production and including my own ethnographic insights in these debates, I argued that a focus on the mobile dimensions of culture aims to unsettle "culture" as something rooted in space and time and to show how people's lives dwell in transit. Like other ethnographers, my interest in the movements of people and ideas within, across, and beyond societal territories invokes various spatial and temporal processes, flows, and fluidities. I suggested, however, that such a focus on movement is not straightforward. It calls for the use of distinct metaphors of movement, especially of travel, migration, and transit. It also requires researchers to be sensitive to various aspects of mobility that pervade the life of stories, events, and places. In elaborating this methodological orientation, I related my own "field" stories of migration and transition with those of other researchers to show the interrelations of space and time, memory and longing, and the local and the global. As suggested, attending to mobility has the potential to undermine the boundaries and borders that confine research to objects, enclosed spaces, and uniform populations. But it also has the potential to keep open the wide range of social practices, tales, and events that distinguish lives in transit. As one method of cultural production designed to overcome the limitations associated with settling people and their practices, it points toward a fluid form of ethnographic research that allows for dimensions of change and interchange to come more sharply into view.

In contemporary times, people, households, labor, information, and images are increasingly in transit as a consequence of different configurations of interstate governance, labor migration, exile patterns, mass tourism, and the tangled relationships of exchange in advanced liberalism and postcolonialism. While such mobile populations and relations are significant in producing new dimensions of social and cultural life, I have been interested in a particular type of diaspora, namely those dispersed peoples who find themselves in border relations with homelands made possible by international labor migration. In this regard, chapter 4 focused on the diasporic relations of the post–World War II guest workers in Western Europe. The guest worker system in Germany involved practices of recruiting workers to the host country, bilateral agreements between Germany and the sending countries, and the regulation of guest workers through policies and programs. The largest group of guest workers in Western Europe since the early 1960s were Turks who migrated at a time when the Turkish state and economy were facing economic and political crises. As a consequence of the perceived unruliness of such diasporic groups, the German state undertook several initiatives to direct their movements within and out of Germany. Similar to other diasporas, the Turkish diaspora were controlled through residential and work permits, immigration policies, naturalization laws based upon descent, and a series of individualizing terms that contributed to their further marginalization in the social, political, and economic affairs of their host country. Occupying a field wherein the importance of national belonging becomes paramount, their cultural distinction as Turkish diaspora is echoed in personal and poetic descriptions of their location in *gurbet*, that is, in their perceived state of exile. Based upon a wide array of diasporic articulations—from state policies to control "foreign" populations, to the words and expressions of guest workers and of *gastarbeiter* literary works—diasporas do not develop from a loss of roots in a community, nor do they develop as a consequence of individuals or groups in solitude. Instead, diasporas are constituted through combined cultural and political processes of migration and "othering" that in turn contribute to a further understanding of the longing in belonging people experience in homelands.

In addition to those diasporas created through patterns of international labor migration, there are other dispersed peoples who find themselves in border relations with homelands and who experience a longing in belonging. While many different kinds of displaced peoples have been created through diverse mobilities, I have been interested in those dispersed peoples who lived in another homeland and returned "home" only to be perceived as foreigners once again. The specific group that I studied were the ethnic Turks from Bulgaria who, with the encouragement of the newly formed Turkish nation-state, emigrated to Turkey during the 1930s. Their emigration was expedited throughout the interwar years by the signing of a convention between Turkey and Bulgaria in 1925. Like the Turkish diaspora in Germany, this group lives in an in-between place that often conjures feelings of homelessness at home and experiences of transit and transition. As I discussed in chapter 5, a number of people from this diasporic group landed in the small community of Arzu in northwestern Turkey located in the inland region of Trakya. From within this ethnographic field, I examined various dimensions of their resettlement. This local site became a focal point in the study of diaspora because it was here that various social, political, economic, and cultural dimensions and tensions of resettlement were played out in the lived experience of local belongings. Although their return home was backed by state resettlement initiatives, the migration of members into this community created tensions between those who consider themselves "locals" and attached to this place and those whose arrival was more recent. Through ethnographic research, I explored these relations of diaspora specific to this "homeland." These relations were elaborated through tales of migration, hardship, and group experiences of the politics of belonging. These stories of diaspora and the practices of resettlement provide valuable insights into the social history and politics of a place, including the ways in which experiences of risk, uncertainty, and insecurity traveled through and permeated the markings of landscapes and the making of lives in transit. These stories of diaspora record unrecorded events. They provided readers with a sense of the complex and the ironic spaces of order, practices of sharing, and fields of work, and with an understanding of locality shaped by contestations within and between regional and national settings. On the margins of these stories, I explored the various ways in which my embodied presence and ethnographic practice shaped the telling of these tales. More like following a flow than pursuing a ready-made route, I found myself susceptible to the movements of branching and forking that pass through diverse stories, commentaries, and conversations and found it essential to negotiate, at every intersection, the path these dialogues would take. This negotiation process reveals, among other things, the complex role of research practices in producing the text.

Partly as a consequence of the expanded mobility of peoples and the shifting of settled boundaries, the ideas and practices associated with belonging are under constant challenge. The home is one of many sites for exploring the challenges to belonging. This is especially so given its connotations as the origin of security, stability, and identity. For some, however, the home has also been mobilized as a terrain of conflict. The conventional understanding of women's place in the "developing" world has adopted a view of households as sites of gender politics, where relations of hierarchy and authority place women as "subjects" of this disciplinary social space. However, given that there has been little research on how women reappropriate these social spaces, I have attended to the ways in which women mobilize and transform their place of dwelling. The point is that women are not simply the passive subjects of household space, its timetables, and its routines, but that through their collective and recollective strategies they also create a space and time for themselves. Through such mobile strategies—not always known in advance or self-present to others—women have the potential to reconstitute their lives outside of these institutional arrangements. In light of these issues, in chapter 6, I showed how rural women in Arzu devised alternative relations of belonging. This inquiry establishes the shifting, theoretical boundaries that encourage us to think not only about the movement of our ideas but also about the attractions of movement for women. The settled space of households is a site of duty that regulates women's time because of the caring, feeding, and reproduction of household members as well as the production and consumption of household goods. In the same alternating space, women also shift from regulated activities and authoritarian relations and create marginal spaces from which to speak the unspoken, tell stories, and invoke change. I suggested that this shift calls for the invention of particular relations, where other geographies and forms of agency can be engendered. In this transgressive context, women's mobile or nomadic encounters produce new perceptions of and possibilities for material life. These effects were especially relevant for those who entered into households from the "outside" and established mobile coalitions with others. These nomadic themes, depicted through women's alternative forms of belonging and their diverse stories of displacement, emphasize the ongoing practice of unsettling and resettling the terrain and the practices of the social by those engaged in the politics of settlement.

REFERENCES

Abadan-Unat, N. 1982. "The Effect of International Migration on Women's Roles: The Turkish Case." In *Sex Roles, Family and Community in Turkey*, ed. C. Kağıtçıbaşı, 207–236. Bloomington: Indiana University Turkish Studies.

Abdo, N. 1994. "Nationalism and Feminism: Palestinian Women and the *Intifada*—No Going Back?" In *Gender and National Identity*, ed. V. Moghadam, 148–170. London: Zed Books.

Abu-Lughod, L. 1993. *Writing Women's Worlds: Bedouin Stories*. Berkeley: University of California Press.

Ahmad, F. 1993. *The Making of Modern Turkey*. London and New York: Routledge.

Ahmed, L. 1982. "Feminism and Feminist Movements in the Middle East, A Preliminary Exploration: Turkey, Egypt, Algeria, People's Democratic Republic of Yemen." *Women's Studies International Forum*, 5 (2): 153–168.

Aleinikoff, A. 1995. "State-Centred Refugee Law: From Resettlement to Containment." In *Mistrusting Refugees*, eds. V. Daniel and J. Knudsen, 257–278. Berkeley and Los Angeles: University of California Press.

Anderson, B. 1983. *Imagined Communities: Reflections on the Origin and Spread of Nationalism*. London: Verso.

Anderson, P. 1991. "Nation-States and National Identity." *London Review of Books* (May 9): 3–8.

Anthias, F., and N. Yuval-Davis. 1989. Introduction to *Women-Nation-State*, eds. N. Yuval-Davis and F. Anthias, 1–15. London: Macmillan.

Anzaldúa, G. 1987. *Borderlands/La Frontera: The New Mestiza*. San Francisco: Spinsters/Aunt Lute.

Appadurai, A. 1996. *Modernity at Large: Cultural Dimensions of Globalization*. Minneapolis: University of Minnesota Press.

Arat, N. 1996. "Women's Studies in Turkey." *Women's Studies Quarterly* 1–2: 400–411.

Arat, Y. 1997. "The Project of Modernity and Women in Turkey." In *Rethinking Modernity and National Identity in Turkey*, eds. S. Bozdoğan and R. Kasaba, 95–112. Seattle and London: University of Washington Press.

———. 1996. "On Gender and Citizenship in Turkey." *Middle East Report* (January–March): 28–31.

Arat, Z. 1994. "Kemalism and Turkish Women." *Women and Politics* 14 (4): 57–80.

Aswad, B. 1974. "Visiting Patterns among Women of the Elite in a Small Turkish City." *Anthropological Quarterly* 47: 9–27.

Atalık, G., and B. Beeley. 1993. "What Mass Migration Has Meant for Turkey." In *Mass Migration in Europe*, ed. R. King, 156–173. New York and Toronto: John Wiley and Sons.

Atatürk, K. 1952. *Atatürk'ün Söylev ve Demeçleri* (Atatürk's Speeches and Statements). Vol. 2. Ankara: Türk Inkilap Tarihi Enstitüsü.

Aucoin, P. 2000. "Blinding the Snake: Women's Myths as Insubordinate Discourse in Western Fiji." *Anthropologica* 42 (1): 11–27.

Bakhtin, M. 1981. *The Dialogic Imagination.* Austin: University of Texas Press.

Barrett, M. 1999. *Imagination in Theory: Culture, Writing, Words, and Things.* Washington Square: New York University Press.

Barrett, M., and A. Phillips. 1992. Introduction to *Destabilizing Theory: Contemporary Feminist Debates*, eds. M. Barrett and A. Phillips, 1–9. Stanford, Calif.: Stanford University Press.

Bauman, Z. 2001a. *The Individualized Society.* Cambridge: Polity Press.

———. 2001b. *Community: Seeking Safety in an Insecure World.* Cambridge, UK: Polity Press.

———. 2000. *Liquid Modernity.* Cambridge: Polity Press.

———. 1999. *In Search of Politics.* Stanford, Calif.: Stanford University Press.

———. 1992. "Soil, Blood and Identity." *The Sociological Review* 40 (4): 675–700.

Baykan, A. 1992. "Women between Fundamentalism and Modernity." In *Theories of Modernity and Postmodernity*, ed. B. Turner, 136–146. London: Stage Publications.

Behar, R. 1996. *The Vulnerable Observer.* Boston: Beacon Press.

Bell, V. 1994. "Dreaming and Time in Foucault's Philosophy." *Theory, Culture & Society* 11:151–163.

Bendix, J. 1985. "On the Rights of Foreign Workers in West Germany." In *Turkish Workers in Europe*, eds. I. Başgöz and N. Furniss, 23–56. Bloomington: Indiana University Press.

Benedict, P. 1974. "The Kabul Günü: Structured Visiting in an Anatolian Provincial Town." *Anthropological Quarterly* 47: 28–47.

Berberoğlu, B. 1991. "Nationalism and Ethnic Rivalry in the Early Twentieth Century: Focus on the Armenian Community in Ottoman Turkey." *Nature, Society, and Thought* 4 (3): 269–301.

———. 1982. *Turkey in Crisis.* London: Zed Press.

Birtek, F., and C. Keyder. 1975. "Agriculture and the State: An Inquiry into Agricultural Differentiation and Political Alliances, The Case of Turkey." *Journal of Peasant Studies* 2 (4): 446–467.

Blunt, A., and G. Rose, eds. 1994. *Writing Women and Space: Colonial and Postcolonial Geographies*. New York and London: Guilford Press.

Borneman, J. 1999. "State, Territory, and National Identity Formation in the Two Berlins, 1945–1995." In *Culture, Power, Place: Explorations in Critical Anthropology*, eds. A. Gupta and J. Ferguson, 93–117. Durham, N.C., and London: Duke University Press.

Bouatta, C. 1994. "Feminine Militancy: *Moudjahidates* during and after the Algerian War." In *Gender and National Identity*, ed. V. Moghadam, 18–39. London: United Nations University.

Bourdieu, P. 1993. *The Field of Cultural Production*. New York: Columbia University Press.

Bozdoğan, S. 1997. "The Predicament of Modernism in Turkish Architectural Culture: An Overview." In *Rethinking Modernity and National Identity in Turkey*, eds. S. Bozdoğan and R. Kasaba, 133–156. Seattle: University of Washington Press.

Brah, A. 1991. "Difference, Diversity and Differentiation." *International Review of Sociology* 2:53–72.

Braidotti, R. 1994. *Nomadic Subjects*. New York: Columbia University Press.

Bridgman, R., S. Cole, and H. Howard-Bobiwash, eds. 1999. *Feminist Fields: Ethnographic Insights*. Peterborough, Ontario: Broadview Press.

Brodie, J. 2000a. "Globalization and the Political Economy of Insecurity." Paper prepared for the Conference "Conceptual Dimensions-Martial Ecologies" Jaffe Centre and Cummings Centre, Tel Aviv University, Israel, May.

———2000b. "Imaging Democratic Urban Citizenship." In *Democracy, Citizenship and the Global City*, ed. E. Isin, 110–128. London: Routledge.

Carnoy, M. 2000. *Sustaining the New Economy: Work, Family, and Community in the Information Age*. New York, NY: Russell Sage Foundation.

Castles, S., and M. Miller. 1998. *The Age of Migration: International Population Movements in the Modern World*. New York and London: Guilford Press.

Chambers, I. 1994. *Migrancy, Culture, Identity*. London: Routledge.

Chatterjee, P. 1986. *Nationalist Thought and the Colonial World*. London: Zed Books.

Chavez, L. 2001. *Covering Immigration: Popular Images and the Politics of the Nation*. Berkeley and Los Angeles, CA: University of California Press.

Cheah, P. 1999. "Spectral Nationality: The Living-On [sur-vie] of the Postcolonial Nation in Neocolonial Globalization." In *Becomings: Explorations in Time, Memory, and Futures*, ed. E. Grosz, 176–200. Ithaca and London: Cornell University Press.

Chow, R. 1993. *Writing Diaspora: Tactics of Intervention in Contemporary Cultural Studies*. Bloomington and Indianapolis: Indiana University Press.

Çinar, D. 1994. "From Aliens to Citizens: A Comparative Analysis of Rules of Transition." In *From Aliens to Citizens: Redefining the Status of Immigrants in Europe*, ed. R. Bauböck, 49–72. Aldershot, England: Avebury.

Clifford, J. 1997. *Routes: Travel and Translation in the Late Twentieth Century*. Cambridge and London: Harvard University Press.

———. 1994. "Diasporas." *Cultural Anthropology*, 9 (3): 302–338.

Cockburn, C. 1998. *The Space between Us: Negotiating Gender and National Identities in Conflict*. London: Zed Books.

Cole, S. 1999. "Pilgram Souls, Honorary Men, (Un)Dutiful Daughters: Sojourners in Modernist Anthropology" In *Feminist Fields: Ethnographic Insights*, eds. R. Bridgman, S. Cole, and H. Howard-Bobiwash, 13–32. Peterborough, Ontario: Broadview Press.

———. 1998. "Reconstituting Households, Retelling Culture: Emigration and Portuguese Fisheries Workers. In *Transgressing Borders: Critical Perspectives on Gender, Household, and Culture*, ed. S. Ilcan and L. Phillips, 75–92. Westport, Conn.: Bergin and Garvey.

———. 1995. "Ruth Landes and the Early Ethnography of Race and Gender." In *Women Writing Culture*, eds. R. Behar and D. Gordon, 166–185. Berkeley: University of California Press.

———. 1992. "Anthropological Lives: The Reflexive Tradition in a Social Science." In *Essays on Life Writing: From Genre to Critical Practice*, ed. M. Kadar, 131–151. Toronto: University of Toronto Press.

———. 1991. *Women of the Praia: Work and Lives in a Portuguese Coastal Community*. Princeton, New Jersey: Princeton University Press.

Delaney, C. 1994. "Untangling the Meanings of Hair in Turkish Society." *Anthropological Quarterly* 67 (4): 159–172.

———. 1991. *Seed and Soil: Gender and Cosmology in Turkish Village Society*. Berkeley: University of California Press.

———. 1990. "The Hajj: Sacred and Secular." *American Ethnologist* 17 (3): 513–530.

Diken, B. 1998. *Strangers, Ambivalence and Social Theory*. Aldershot, England: Ashgate.

Doomernik, J. 1995. "The Institutionalization of Turkish Islam in Germany and the Netherlands: A Comparison." *Ethnic and Racial Studies* 8 (1): 46–63.

Dossa, P. 1999. "Narrating Embodied Lives: Muslim Women on the Coast of Kenya." In *Feminist Fields: Ethnographic Insights*, eds. R. Bridgman, S. Cole, and H. Howard-Bobiwash, 157–172. Peterborough, Ontario: Broadview Press.

The Economist. 2000. "Turkey: Atatürk's Long Shadow." 10–16: June: 1–18.

Enloe, C. 1989. *Bananas, Beaches and Bases: Making Feminist Sense of International Politics*. London: Pandora.

Erdentuğ, A., and B. Burçak. 1998. "Political Tuning in Ankara, a Capital, As Reflected in Its Urban Symbols and Images." *International Journal of Urban and Regional Research* 22 (4): 589–601.

Erman, T. 1997. "The Meaning of City Living for Rural Migrant Women and Their Role in Migration: The Case of Turkey." *Women's Studies International Forum* 20 (2): 263–273.

Ertem, G. 1999. "Off the Feminist Platform in Turkey: Cherkess Gender Relations." In *Feminist Fields: Ethnographic Insights*, eds. R. Bridgman, S. Cole, and H. Howard-Bobiwash, 173–195. Peterborough, Ontario: Broadview Press.

Fassmann, H., and R. Münz. 1994. "European East–West Migration, 1945–1992." *International Migration Review* 28 (3): 520–538.

Ferguson, J. 1999. "The Country and the City on the Copperbelt." In *Culture,*

Power, Place: Explorations in Critical Anthropology, eds. A. Gupta and J. Ferguson, 137–154. Durham, N.C., and London: Duke University Press.

Fischer, M. 1995. "Starting Over: How, What, and For Whom Does One Write about Refugees? The Poetics and Politics of Refugee Film as Ethnographic Access in a Media-Saturated World." In *Mistrusting Refugees*, eds. V. Daniel and J. Knudsen, 126–150. Berkeley and Los Angeles: University of California Press.

Foucault, M. 1979. *Discipline and Punish: The Birth of the Prison*. New York: Vintage Books.

Gaiskell, D., and E. Unterhaulter. 1989. "Mothers of a Nation: A Comparative Analysis of Nation, Race and Motherhood in Afrikaner Nationalism and the African National Congress." In *Women-Nation-State*, eds. N. Yuval-Davis and F. Anthias. London: Macmillan.

Ganguly, K. 1992. "Migrant Identities: Personal Memory and the Construction of Selfhood." *Cultural Studies* 6 (1): 27–50.

Gelvin, J. 1998. *Divided Loyalties: Nationalism and Mass Politics in Syria at the Close of Empire*. Berkeley and Los Angeles: University of California Press.

Ghorayshi, P. 1998. "Rural Women Face Capitalism: Women's Response as 'Guardians' of the Household." In *Transgressing Borders: Critical Perspectives on Gender, Household, and Culture*, eds. S. Ilcan and L. Phillips, 189–207. Westport, Conn.: Bergin and Garvey.

Giddens, A. 1994. *Beyond Left and Right: The Future of Radical Politics*. Stanford, Calif.: Stanford University Press.

Gilroy, P. 1993. *The Black Atlantic: Modernity and Double Consciousness*. Cambridge: Harvard University Press.

Gitmez, A. 1979. *Dişgöç Oyküşü*. Ankara: Maya Matbaacilik Yayincilik.

Göçek, M., and S. Balaghi. 1994. "Reconstructing Gender in the Middle East through Voice and Experience." In *Reconstructing Gender in the Middle East*, eds. M. Göçek and S. Balaghi, 1–19. New York: Columbia University Press.

Göle, N. 1997. "The Gendered Nature of the Public Sphere." *Public Culture* 10 (1): 61–81.

———. 1996. *The Forbidden Modern: Civilization and Veiling*. Ann Arbor: University of Michigan Press.

———. 1991. *Modern Mahrem: Medeniyet ve Örtünme*. Istanbul: Metis Yayinlari.

Gordon, D. 1968. *Women of Algeria: An Essay on Change*. Middle Eastern Monograph Series. Cambridge: Harvard University Press.

Grossberg, L. 1996. "The Space of Culture, the Power of Space." In *The Post-Colonial Question: Common Skies, Divided Horizons*, eds. I. Chambers and L. Curti, 169–188. London and New York: Routledge.

Grosz, E. 1995. *Space, Time, and Perversion: Essays on the Politics of Bodies*. London: Routledge.

———. 1993. "Judaism and Exile: The Ethics of Otherness." In *Space & Place: Theories of Identity and Location*, eds. E. Carter, J. Donald, and J. Squires, 55–71. London: Lawrence & Wishart.

Gülalp, H. 1994. "Capitalism and the Modern Nation-State: Rethinking the Creation of the Turkish Republic." *Journal of Historical Sociology* 7 (2): 155–176.

———. 1985. "Patterns of Capital Accumulation and State–Society Relations in Turkey." *Journal of Contemporary Asia* 15 (3): 329–348.

Gupta, A. 1999. "The Song of the Nonaligned World: Transnational Identities and the Reinscription of Space in Late Capitalism." In *Culture, Power, Place: Explorations in Critical Anthropology*, eds. A. Gupta and J. Ferguson, 179–199. Durham, N.C., and London: Duke University Press.

Gupta, A., and J. Ferguson. 1999a. "Culture, Power, Place: Ethnography at the End of an Era." In *Culture, Power, Place: Explorations in Critical Anthropology*, eds. A. Gupta and J. Ferguson, 1–29. Durham and London: Duke University Press.

———. 1999b. "Beyond Culture: Space, Identity, and the Politics of Difference." In *Culture, Power, Place: Explorations in Critical Anthropology*, eds. A. Gupta and J. Ferguson, 33–51. Durham, N.C., and London: Duke University Press.

Halman, T. S. 1985. "Big Town Blues: Peasants 'Abroad' in Turkish Literature." In *Turkish Workers in Europe*, eds. I. Başgöz and N. Furniss, 81–102. Bloomington: Indiana University Press.

Hanson, S., and G. Pratt. 1995. *Gender, Work, and Space*. London and New York: Routledge.

Hobsbawn, E., and T. Ranger. 1983. *The Invention of Tradition*. Cambridge: Cambridge University Press.

Holy, L. 1998. "The Metaphor of 'Home' in Czech Nationalist Discourse." In *Migrants of Identity: Perceptions of Home in a World of Movement*, eds. N. Rapport and A. Dawson, 111–137. Oxford and New York: Berg.

hooks, b. 1990. *Yearning: Race, Gender, and Cultural Politics*. Boston: South End Press.

Ifekwunigwe, J. 1999. *Scattered Belongings: Cultural Paradoxes of "Race," Nation and Gender*. London and New York: Routledge.

Ignatieff, M. 1993. *Blood and Belonging: Journeys into the New Nationalism*. New York: Farrar, Straus & Giroux.

Ilcan, S. 1998a. "Occupying the Margins: On Spacing Gender and Gendering Space." *Space and Culture* 3:5–26.

———. 1998b. "Challenging Settlement: Women's Culture of Dis-placement." In *Transgressing Borders: Critical Perspectives on Gender, Household, and Culture*, eds. S. Ilcan and L. Phillips, 55–73. Westport, Conn.: Bergin and Garvey.

———. 1996a. "Fragmentary Encounters in a Moral World." *Ethnology* 35 (1): 33–49.

———. 1996b. "Moral Regulation and Microlevel Politics: Implications for Women's Work and Struggles." In *Women, Work and Gender Relations in Developing Countries*, eds. P. Ghorayshi and C. Belanger, 115–131. Westport, Conn.: Greenwood Press.

———. 1994. "Peasant Struggles and Social Change: Migration, Households, and Gender in Rural Turkish Society." *International Migration Review* 28 (3): 554–579.

Ilcan, S., and L. Phillips. 2000. "Mapping Populations: The United Nations, Globalization, and Engendered Spaces." *Alternatives* 25 (4): 467–489.

Incirlioğlu, E. O. 1993. "Marriage, Gender Relations and Rural Transformation in

Central Anatolia." In *Culture and Economy: Changes in Turkish Villages*, ed. P. Stirling, 115–125. Cambridgeshire: Eothen Press.

Isin, E. 2000. "Introduction: Democracy, Citizenship and the City." In *Democracy, Citizenship and the Global City*, ed. E. Isin, 1–21. London: Routledge.

Jameson, F., and M. Miyoshi, eds. 1999. *The Cultures of Globalization*. Durham and London: Duke University Press.

Jansen, S. 1998. "Homeless at Home: Narratives of Post-Yugoslav Identities." In *Migrants of Identity: Perceptions of Home in a World of Movement*, eds. N. Rapport and A. Dawson, 85–109. Oxford and New York: Berg.

Jayawardena, K. 1986. *Feminism and Nationalism in the Third World*. London: Zed Books.

Jenks, C. 1995. "The Centrality of the Eye in Western Culture: An Introduction." In *Visual Culture*, ed. C. Jenks, 1–25. London and New York: Routledge.

Kağıtçıbaşı, C. 1985. "Immigrant Populations in Europe: Problems Viewed from the Sending Country." In *Turkish Workers in Europe*, eds. I. Başgöz and N. Furniss, 103–123. Bloomington: Indiana University Turkish Studies.

Kandiyoti, D. 1997. "Gendering the Modern: On Missing Dimensions in the Study of Turkish Modernity." In *Rethinking Modernity and National Identity in Turkey*, eds. S. Bozdoğan and R. Kasaba, 113–132. Seattle: University of Washington Press.

———. 1991. "End of Empire: Islam, Nationalism and Women in Turkey." In *Women, Islam, and the State*, ed. D. Kandiyoti, 22–47. Philadelphia: Temple University Press.

Kaplan, C. 1998. *Questions of Travel*. Durham, N.C., and London: Duke University Press.

Kesaba, R. 1997. "Kemalist Certainties and Modern Ambiguities." In *Rethinking Modernity and National Identity in Turkey*, eds. S. Bozdoğan and R. Kasaba, 15–36. Seattle: University of Washington Press.

Keyder, C. 1987. *State and Class in Turkey*. London: Verso.

———. 1983. "Paths of Rural Transformation in Turkey." *Journal of Peasant Studies* 11 (1): 34–49.

Khouri, D. 1996. "Drawing Boundaries and Defining Spaces: Women and Space in Ottoman Iraq." In *Women, the Family, and Divorce Laws in Islamic History*, ed. A. Sonbol, 173–187. Syracuse, N.Y.: Syracuse University Press.

Kiray, M. 1976. "The Family of the Immigrant Worker." In *Turkish Workers in Europe, 1960–1975*, ed. N. Abadan-Unat. Leiden: E. J. Brill.

Kirby, K. 1993. "Thinking Through the Boundary: The Politics of Location, Subjects, and Space." *boundary 2*, 20 (2): 173–189.

Knauss, P. 1987. *The Persistence of Patriarchy: Class, Gender and Ideology in Twentieth Century Algeria*. New York: Praeger.

Kocturk, T. 1992. *A Matter of Honour: Experiences of Turkish Women Immigrants*. London and Atlantic Highlands: Zed Books.

Kristeva, J. 1991. *Strangers to Ourselves*. New York: Columbia University Press.

Lefebvre, H. 1991. *The Production of Space*. Trans. Donald Nicholson-Smith. Oxford and Cambridge: Blackwell.

Leonard, K. 1999. "Finding One's Own Place: Asian Landscapes Re-visioned in Rural California." In *Culture, Power, Place: Explorations in Critical An-*

thropology, eds. A. Gupta and J. Ferguson, 118–136. Durham N.C., and London: Duke University Press.

Let's Go: The Budget Guide to Greece and Turkey. 1994. New York: St. Martin's Press.

Lewis, B. 1968. *Emergence of Modern Turkey.* 2nd ed. New York: Oxford University Press.

Lovell, N., ed. 1998. *Locality and Belonging.* London: Routledge.

Malkki, L. 1999. "National Geographic: The Rooting of Peoples and the Territorialization of National Identity among Scholars and Refugees." In *Culture, Power, Place: Explorations in Critical Anthropology*, eds. A. Gupta and J. Ferguson, 52–74. Durham, N.C., and London: Duke University Press.

Marcus, G. 1989. "Imagining the Whole: Ethnography's Contemporary Efforts to Situate Itself." *Critique of Anthropology* 9 (3): 7–30.

McClintock, A. 1997. "No Longer in a Future Heaven: Gender, Race, and Nationalism." In *Dangerous Liasons: Gender, Nation, and Postcolonial Perspectives*, eds. A. McClintock, A. Mufti, and E. Shohat, 89–112. Minneapolis and London: University of Minnesota Press.

———. 1993. "Family Feuds: Gender, Nationalism and the Family." *Feminist Review* 44:61–80.

Melman, B. 1996. "Transparent Veils: Western Women Dis-Orient the East." In *The Geography of Identity*, ed. P. Yaeger, 433–465. Ann Arbor: University of Michigan Press.

Meneley, A. 2000. "Living Hierarchy in Yemen." *Anthropologica* 42 (1): 61–73.

Minh-ha, T. 1994. "Other Than Myself/My Other Self." In *Travellers' Tales: Narratives of Home and Displacement*, eds. G. Robertson, et al., 9–26. London and New York: Routledge.

———. 1993. "All-Owning Spectatorship." In *Feminism and the Politics of Difference*, eds. S. Gunew and A. Yeatman, 157–176. Halifax, Nova Scotia: Fernwood.

———. 1991. *When the Moon Waxes Red.* London: Routledge.

Moghadam, V., ed. 1994. *Gender and National Identity.* London: United Nations University.

———. 1993. *Modernizing Women: Gender and Social Change in the Middle East.* Boulder, Colo., and London: Lynne Rienner.

Moore, H. 1994. *A Passion for Difference.* Bloomington and Indianapolis: Indiana University Press.

Mouffe, C. 1994. "For a Politics of Nomadic Identity." In *Travellers' Tales: Narratives of Home and Displacement*, eds. G. Robertson et al., 105–113. London and New York: Routledge.

Mushaben, J. 1985. "A Crisis of Culture: Isolation and Integration among Turkish Guestworkers in the German Federal Republic." In *Turkish Workers in Europe*, eds. I. Başgöz and N. Furniss, 125–150. Bloomington: Indiana University Press.

Nagel, J. 1998. "Masculinity and Nationalism: Gender and Sexuality in the Making of Nations." *Ethnic and Racial Studies* 21 (2): 242–263.

Najmabadi, A. 1993. "Veiled Discourse—Unveiled Bodies." *Feminist Studies* 3: 487–518.

Olson, E. 1985. "Muslim Identity and Secularism in Contemporary Turkey: The Headscarf Dispute."*Anthropological Quarterly* 58 (6): 161–171.

Olwig, K. F. 1997. "Cultural Sites: Sustaining a Home in a Deterritorialized World." In *Siting Culture: The Shifting Anthropological Object*, eds. K. F. Olwig and K. Hastrup, 17–38. London and New York: Routledge.

Ong, A. 1995. "Women Out of China: Traveling Tales and Traveling Theories in Postcolonial Feminism." In *Women Writing Culture*, eds. R. Behar and D. Gordon, 350–372. Berkeley: University of California Press.

Orga, I. 1988. *Portrait of a Turkish Family*. London: Eland.

Özdamar, E. S. 1994. *Mother Tongue*. Trans. Craig Thomas. Toronto: Coach House Press.

Öztürkmen, A. 1994. "The Role of People's Houses in the Making of National Culture in Turkey." *New Perspectives on Turkey* 11:159–181.

Paine, S. 1974. *Exporting Workers: The Turkish Case*. London and New York: Cambridge University Press.

Peck, J. 1995. "Refugees as Foreigners: The Problem of Becoming German and Finding a Home." In *Mistrusting Refugees*, eds. E. Valentine Daniel and J. Knudsen, 102–125. Berkeley and Los Angeles: University of California Press.

Penninx, R. 1982. "A Critical Review of Theory and Practice: The Case of Turkey." *International Migration Review* 16 (4): 781–818.

Phillips, L. 1998. "Dissecting Globalization: Women's Space-Time in the Other America." In *Transgressing Borders: Critical Perspectives on Gender, Household, and Culture*, eds. S. Ilcan and L. Phillips, 37–53. Westport, Conn.: Bergin and Garvey.

———. 1996. "Toward Postcolonial Methodologies." In *Women, Work, and Gender Relations in Developing Countries*, eds. P. Ghorayshi and C. Belanger, 15–29. Westport, Conn.: Greenwood Press.

Phillips, L., and S. Ilcan. 2000. "Domesticating Spaces in Transition: Politics and Practices in the Gender and Development Literature, 1970–99." *Anthropologica* 42 (2): 205–216.

Probyn, E. 1999. "Bloody Metaphors and Other Allegories of the Ordinary." In *Between Woman and Nation*, eds. C. Kaplan, N. Alarcón, and M. Moallem, 47–62. Durham N.C., and London: Duke University Press.

———. 1996. *Outside Belongings*. New York and London: Routledge.

Rapport, N., and A. Dawson, eds. 1998. *Migrants of Identity: Perceptions of Home in a World of Movement*. Oxford and New York: Berg.

Razack, S. 1996. "The Perils of Storytelling for Refugee Women." In *Development and Diaspora: Gender and the Refugee Experience*, eds. W. Giles, H. Moussa, and P. Van Esterik, 164–174. Dundas, Ontario: Artemis Enterprises.

Ricoeur, P. 1979. "The Model of the Text: Meaningful Action Considered As a Text." In *Interpretive Social Science: A Reader*, eds. P. Rabinow and W. Sullivan, 73–101. Berkeley: University of California Press.

Rittstieg, H. 1994. "Dual Citizenship: Legal and Political Aspects in the German Context." In *From Aliens to Citizens: Redefining the Status of Immigrants in Europe*, ed. R. Bauböck, 111–120. Aldershot, England: Avebury.

Rodríguez, I. 1994. *House/Garden/Nation*. Durham, N.C., and London: Duke University Press.

Rose, N. 1999. *Powers of Freedom: Reframing Political Thought.* Cambridge: Cambridge University Press.

Rose, N., and P. Miller. 1992. "Political Power Beyond the State: Problematics of Government." *British Journal of Sociology* 43 (2): 173–205.

Rothenburg, C. 1999. "Who Are We for Them? On Doing Research in the Palestinian West Bank." In *Feminist Fields: Ethnographic Insights*, eds. R. Bridgman, S. Cole, and H. Howard-Bobiwash, 137–156. Peterborough, Ontario: Broadview Press.

Rushdie, S. 1984. *Shame.* London: Picador.

Safran, W. 1991. "Diasporas in Modern Societies: Myths of Homeland and Return." *Diaspora* 1 (1): 83–99.

Said, E. 1978. *Orientalism.* New York: Pantheon.

Salazar, C. 1991. "A Third World Woman's Text: Between the Politics of Criticism and Cultural Politics." In *Women's Words: The Feminist Practice of Oral History*, eds. S. Berger Gluck and D. Patai, 93–106. New York and London: Routledge.

Salt, J. 1995. "Nationalism and the Rise of Muslim Sentiment." *Middle Eastern Studies* 31 (1): 13–27.

Sassen, S. 1998. *Globalization and Its Discontents: Essays on the New Mobility of People and Money.* New York: New Press.

Shields, R. 1999. "Culture and the Economy of Cities." *European Urban and Regional Studies* 6 (4): 303–311.

Simmel, G. 1950. *The Sociology of Georg Simmel.* Trans. and ed. K. Wolff. New York: Free Press.

Sirman, N. 1991. "Friend or Foe? Forging Alliances with Other Women in a Village of Western Turkey." In *Women in Modern Turkish Society*, ed. S. Tekeli, 199–218. London and New York City: Zed Books.

———. 1990. "State, Village and Gender in Western Turkey." In *Turkish State, Turkish Society*, eds. A. Finkel and N. Sirman, 21–52. London and New York: Routledge.

Stacey, J. 1991. "Can There Be a Feminist Ethnography?" In *Women's Words: The Feminist Practice of Oral History*, eds. S. Berger Gluck and D. Patai, 111–120. New York and London: Routledge.

Starr, J. 1989. "The Role of Turkish Secular Law in Changing the Lives of Rural Muslim Women, 1950–1970." *Law and Society Review* 23 (3): 497–523.

Stasiulis, D. 1999. "Relational Positionalities of Nationalisms, Racisms, and Feminisms." In *Between Woman and Nation*, eds. C. Kaplan, N. Alarcón, and M. Moallem, 182–218. Durham, N.C., and London: Duke University Press.

Stasiulis, D., and N. Yuval-Davis, eds. 1995. *Unsettling Settler Societies: Articulations of Gender, Race, Ethnicity, and Class.* London: Sage.

Stewart, K. 1996. *A Space on the Side of the Road: Cultural Poetics in an "Other" America.* Princeton, N.J.: Princeton University Press.

Stirling, P. 1965. *Turkish Village.* London: Weidenfeld and Nicolson.

Su, K. 1999. "Translating Mother Tongues: Amy Tan and Maxine Hong Kingston on Ethnographic Authority." In *Feminist Fields: Ethnographic Insights*, eds. R. Bridgman, S. Cole, and H. Howard-Bobiwash, 33–53. Peterborough, Ontario: Broadview Press.

Taşkiran, T. 1976. *Women in Turkey.* Istanbul: Redhouse Press.

Taussig, M. 1992. *The Nervous System*. New York: Routledge.

Torpey, J. 2000. *The Invention of the Passport: Surveillance, Citizenship and the State*. Cambridge: Cambridge University Press.

Urry, J. 2000a. *Sociology Beyond Societies: Mobilities for the Twenty-first Century*. London and New York: Routledge.

———. 2000b. "Global Flows and Global Citizenship." In *Democracy, Citizenship and the Global City*, ed. E. Isin, 62–78. London: Routledge.

Van Hear, N. 1998. *New Diasporas: The Mass Exodus, Dispersal and Regrouping of Migrant Communities*. Seattle: University of Washington Press.

Wheatcroft, A. 1995. *The Ottomans: Dissolving Images*. London: Penguin Books.

Wolcott H. 1995. "Making a Study 'More Ethnographic.' " In *Representation in Ethnography*, ed. Van Maanen, 79–111. London: Sage.

Yeğenoğlu, M. 1998. *Colonial Fantasies: Towards a Feminist Reading of Orientalism*. Cambridge: Cambridge University Press.

Yuval-Davis, N. 2000. "Citizenship, Territoriality and the Gendered Construction of Difference." In *Democracy, Citizenship and the Global City*, ed. E. Isin, 171–188. London: Routledge.

———. 1997. *National Spaces and Collective Identities: Borders, Boundaries, Citizenship and Gender Relations*." Inaugural lecture, July. University of Greenwich, London, England.

———. 1993. "Gender and Nation." *Ethnic and Racial Studies* 16 (4): 621–632.

Yuval-Davis, N., and F. Anthias, eds. 1989. *Women-Nation-State*. London: Macmillan.

Zurcher, E. 1993. *Turkey: A Modern History*. London: I. B. Tauris.

INDEX

Abdo, N., 19
Abu-Lughod, L., 6, 9, 40; and the "writing against culture," 100
Afghanistan, 23
Afrikaner women, 23
agriculture. *See* Turkey, and agriculture
Ahmed, L., 19
Alamanian lights, 44
Algeria, and women's role in nation-building, 19–20
Aliens Act (Germany, 1965), 62
Anatolia, 39; and the community of Gökler, 81; and War of national Independence, 15; women in, 24
Anderson, P., 20
Ankara, 22, 26
Appadurai, A., 2, 35, 37, 38–39, 48
Arat, Y., 22
Arzu, 8, 75, 84–86, 91, 99, 102, 104, 105, 119, 120; and agriculture, 103–104; background, 77–78; child rearing in, 95; and industrialization, 80–81; location, 77; and the modern man, 103; and the modern woman, 103–104; neighborhoods, 82–83;

oral history of settlement, 77; poverty of, 79–80; spatial organization of the community, 82–83; and Turkish military mobilization, 78
Atatürk. *See* Kemal, Mustafa
*ausländer(s),*7, 45, 60; other terms for, 63. *See also* Turkish *ausländers*
ausländerpolizei, 61–62
ausländerroboter, 63
ausländische arbeitnehmer, 63
Austria, 57
Awlad 'Ali, 100

Bakhtin, M., 49, 112
Balkan War, 76
Baltics, the, 58
Barthes, R., 49
Bauman, Z., 1, 2, 8, 11, 12, 14, 122
Behar, R., 52
Belgium, 60
Bella, Ben, 19
Bellorussia, 58
belonging, 2–4, 40, 46, 85, 91, 112, 116, 120; alternative relations of, 9; and citizenship, 62–63; longing for, 2, 3–4, 7, 45, 119; movement

"writing against culture," 6, 9, 37, 40,
  50
"writing against writing culture," 37
"writing culture," 42
Writing Women's Worlds (Abu-
  Lughod), 40

Yanomani, 11
Yugoslavia, 59, 61, 91
Yuval-Davis, N., 4, 19, 23, 66

Zonguldak, 67–69, 92

About the Author

SUZAN ILCAN is Canada Research Chair in Social Justice and Globalization and Associate Professor in the Department of Sociology and Anthropology at the University of Windsor. She is Editor of *Transgressing Borders* (with L. Phillips, Bergin & Garvey, 1998). Her current research deals with issues of globalization, national and international agencies, and expert knowledge and governance.